MARK & EMPIRE

MARK & EMPIRE

Feminist Reflections _____

by

Laurel K. Cobb

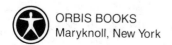

ORBIS BOOKS
Maryknoll, New York

ORBIS BOOKS
Maryknoll, New York 10545

Fathers and Brothers
MARYKNOLL™

Founded in 1970, Orbis Books endeavors to publish works that enlighten the mind, nourish the spirit, and challenge the conscience. The publishing arm of the Maryknoll Fathers and Brothers, Orbis seeks to explore the global dimensions of the Christian faith and mission, to invite dialogue with diverse cultures and religious traditions, and to serve the cause of reconciliation and peace. The books published reflect the views of their authors and do not represent the official position of the Maryknoll Society. To learn more about Maryknoll and Orbis Books, please visit our website at www.maryknollsociety.org.

Published by Orbis Books, Maryknoll, New York 10545-0302.
Manufactured in the United States of America.

Library of Congress Cataloging-in-Publication Data

Cobb, Laurel K.
    Mark and empire : feminist reflections / by Laurel K. Cobb.
        pages cm
    Includes bibliographical references and index.
    ISBN 978-1-62698-047-1 (pbk.)
    1. Bible. Mark—Commentaries. I. Title.
    BS2585.53.C57   2013
    226.3'06—dc23
                                        2013011440

For I am about to create new heavens and a new earth; the former things shall not be remembered or come to mind. But be glad and rejoice forever in what I am creating . . . no more shall the sound of weeping be heard in it, or the cry of distress. No more shall there be in it an infant that lives but a few days, or an old person who does not live out a lifetime. . . .

They shall build houses and inhabit them; they shall plant vineyards and eat their fruit. They shall not build and another inhabit; they shall not plant and another eat; for like the days of a tree shall the days of my people be, and my chosen shall long enjoy the work of their hands. They shall not labor in vain, or bear children for calamity; for they shall be offspring blessed by the Lord—and their descendants as well.

Before they call I will answer, while they are yet speaking I will hear. The wolf and the lamb shall feed together, the lion shall eat straw like the ox. . . . They shall not hurt or destroy on all my holy mountain, says the Lord.

Isaiah 65:17-25

CONTENTS

FOREWORD

The core question of Christian discipleship in every age is: How do we follow Jesus? We can't answer it, however, unless we know *where Jesus was and is* in the real world we inhabit. The problem with much First World Christianity is that the Jesus we talk about doesn't actually dwell in a real world. His story seems to have taken place in a kind of Disneyland, far, far away from landscapes of conflict, poverty, oppression, and war. This is why Jesus' prophetic witness has become so profoundly domesticated in our churches. As Brian McLaren put it so concisely in *Everything Must Change,* "The popular and domesticated Jesus . . . has become little more than a chrome-plated hood ornament on the guzzling Hummer of Western civilization."

The notion that Jesus floats above the world in some spiritual ethersphere is actually the oldest heresy in our tradition, known as Docetism. Docetists didn't like the idea of incarnation, preferring a radical separation of the somatic and historical from the spiritual and divine. Their slogan was: "If Jesus was really human, he could not have been God, and if Jesus was really God, he could not have been human." This perspective was rightly rejected by the early church as heresy. Though the church may have won that battle, however, it lost the war. Because most Christian churches today, at least in the West, are functionally Docetic, believing in a Jesus who lived, died, and was risen *apart* from the real world—especially *ours.* This is why we activist educators have such a difficult time persuading churches to enlist into historic struggles for justice and peace.

In every generation, the best way to combat Docetism is to take a *radical* approach. That is, we must transcend the often dysfunctional superstructures of the institutionalized church to return again and again to the roots of the Christian faith in the gospel. And we must move beyond a cosmetic address of symptomatic problems in order to explore the roots of *our* personal and political pathologies and their impact on real people and places in the real terrain of our history. The hope of the former provides courage for the difficult and demanding work of the latter, and healing and change can result. Indeed, the many and diverse renewal movements in the long (and often apostate) history of Christendom have always had in common two engagements: fresh readings of scripture and solidarity with the poor and marginalized.

In light of this continuing imperative, Mark's Gospel, as the earliest of our stories of Jesus, simply *cannot* be revisited too often by our churches. Its primal narrative comes alive when we read it synoptically with a critical analysis of contemporary empire on one hand, and movements of human healing and liberation on the other—as demonstrated in Laurel Cobb's study guide to Mark.

Torn early on between a call to both seminary and international poverty and justice work, Cobb decided on the latter. For three and a half decades she worked in international public health and social welfare programs in some thirty-five countries in Latin America, Africa, the Middle East, and Asia, including El Salvador, Bangladesh, Sri Lanka, Egypt, Bolivia, and Palestine. With Masters degrees in Social Work and Public Administration, her focus was in maternal and child health, family planning, safe motherhood, child survival, and HIV/AIDS programs with underserved populations. An active mission educator in the United Church of Christ, in retirement Cobb began studies at Andover Newton Theological Seminary, interrupted them for two last assignments in Angola and Uganda, then completed her Masters in Theological Research, which represents the core of this book.

Cobb introduced her thesis with this comment: "The Gospel of Mark brought Jesus alive to me when I read it with a copy of Ched Myers's *Binding the Strong Man: A Political Reading of Mark's Story of Jesus* at my side after working, traveling and living for thirty years in the global inequity of the Two-Thirds World." I am delighted that a quarter century after the publication of my commentary, Orbis is offering *Mark & Empire: Feminist Reflections*, in which Cobb puts Mark in conversation with her long experience of service, advocacy, and solidarity. It is especially fitting that this book emphasizes work with and among women; after all, they were the last ones standing in Mark's narrative of Jesus!

I commend Cobb's reflections to those who desire to "see" in the tradition of the evangelist's story about the blind beggar Bartimaeus (Mark 10:46-52). This vignette, which concludes Mark's masterful "discipleship catechism" (8:22–10:52), "speaks to our condition" (as Quakers say). As persons of relative privilege in the belly of empire, we U.S. Christians struggle to shed our blindness, even as we try to embrace the journey of discipleship. The healing of Bartimaeus suggests that faith ultimately is *not* a matter of cognitive assent, nor of churchly habit, nor of liturgical magic, nor of theological sophistication or doctrinal correctness, nor of religious piety, nor any of the other poor substitutes that we Christians have conjured through the ages. Discipleship is at its core a matter of whether or not we really want to *see* enough to follow Jesus' Way.

First, we must see our weary world as it truly *is*, without denial and delusion: the tough realities and inconvenient truths about economic disparity and racial oppression and ecological destruction and war without end. And then we must see our beautiful world as it truly *could be*, without despair or distraction: God's dream of economic justice for all and beloved community and restored creation and the peaceable kingdom—God's vision of things. For almost four decades I have tried to live *into* Mark's story of Bartimaeus, and I have not grown *out* of its wisdom—such is the power of this Gospel.

Cobb's modest, readable and thoroughly grounded book is ideal for popular study, and I hope it will be taken up by those seeking to effect personal and political change. To be sure, our churches still dwell too easily under the shadow of empire, and those who understand the essential connections between faith and justice are still too few. But as Mark reminds us, in the wilderness, empowered by divine grace, small numbers can multiply like loaves, until Beloved Community abounds. May this study inspire a new generation to follow Mark's Jesus in the Way of love and justice for all.

Ched Myers
Oak View, CA
International Women's Day, 2013

Acknowledgments ⎯⎯⎯⎯⎯⎯⎯⎯⎯

My sincere thanks to Professor William R. Herzog II, my advisor at Andover Newton Theological School, who encouraged and supported my publishing these reflections, to Professor Sharon G. Thornton, who encouraged and modeled "women writing theology," to Professor Mary Luti, whose writings continue to nourish my life, and to all the other wonderful faculty and staff at Andover Newton; to Jim Keane, my supportive editor at Orbis Books, and to the Reverend Duane Clinker, who introduced me to the theology of a "radical Jesus" in the Gospel of Mark and to Ched Myers's writings. My heartfelt thanks to Ched himself for his work, his writings, and his willingness to write a foreword to this book. And most particularly, I thank my marine-biologist husband, Stan, my love and support for more than fifty years.

Introduction

As an American social worker traveling home from Australia in 1977, I awoke from a sound sleep in the back seat of a taxi a few hours outside of Delhi, India, and asked the driver what the smell that had awakened me was. He replied that it was nothing; we had left the city and the smell was just a village around the corner. A minute later and the village was before us: low, mud-brick houses and a small, shallow pond in which women bathed babies and washed dishes; children splashed and played; men took their baths; girls collected drinking water; and water buffalo urinated and defecated. The village's only source of water was this pond. It was a simple sight representing poverty, powerlessness, and inequity. I had seen such villages many times before, as well as the urban poverty of New Delhi and other Asian cities. The sight had become familiar, "normal" even. I had come to regard such poverty and powerlessness as "just the ways things were." That afternoon was different. I saw the village in light of God's world of abundance and grace. My world was turned upside down.

In the Gospel of Mark, blind people gain sight. Many years after my encounter at the pond, reading Mark with a copy of Ched Myers's *Binding the Strong Man*[1] at my side, I recognized myself and our world in Mark's stories of Jesus. The Gospel is a story of justice and love in a world of inequity and oppression, written during the suffering of the Jewish rebellion against the Roman Empire. It is a story of faithfulness and liberation for today.

The challenge of how to live faithfully as a servant of the living God in the context of power, privilege, and inequity is timeless. The face of empire changes over the millennia, but the challenge remains. In the ancient empires of the Old Testament, Israel's God demanded liberation, righteousness, and mercy for the oppressed and vulnerable. Centuries later Jesus, the "pedagogue of the oppressed,"[2] brought renewal

1

to Roman-occupied Israel. In crowds of the exploited and impoverished, he gave voice to the voiceless, sight to the blind, and freedom to the enchained. He healed the daughter of a Gentile woman who crossed gender and cultural barriers to demand compassion. He gave sight to an insistent blind man who cried out for mercy and then followed him. He challenged and threatened the power of religious and political elites who accused him of blasphemy. He threatened mighty Rome itself, who saw him as "King of the Jews." And he died on a cross in the Roman punishment for rebels and revolutionaries.

The story didn't end there. After the crucifixion Jesus was experienced as alive among his followers, who spread across the Roman Empire to share the good news of his life, death, and resurrection. The Gospel was in their heads, hearts, hands, and remembrances and expressions of the meaning of Jesus in the lives of the first individuals and communities who followed him.[3] The Gospel of Mark is good news: empowerment, liberation, wholeness, and hope across the ages and around the globe.

It's needed good news. Geography leaves the majority in the Two-Thirds World in life-long poverty, oppression, and risk while intersections of class, race, and gender create power, privilege, and inequity within the United States. Eighty-five percent of the world's population, the Two-Thirds World of Africa, Asia, and Latin America, receives just 25 percent of total world income. The richest one-third of American households owns 90 percent of all American wealth and holds power and influence proportionately. Those of the Two-Thirds World, like the Indian villagers at their pond, are invisible to most of those in the First World (United States, Canada, Europe, Australia, and Japan). Many of America's poor, in the inner city and in rural hamlets, are also invisible. The inequity that gave rise to the term the "Two-Thirds World" globally is now recognized on our own home soil. Increasingly, however, Americans are recognizing national and global inequity, identifying it as a consequence of empire and defining it as unjust.

We yearn for justice in today's American Empire as peoples did in the Roman Empire. As I write in the first chapters of these reflections, the two empires are similar in their exercise of powers: ideological, economic, political, and military. In the first century, worship of the Roman emperor as divine was the ideological power that held the empire together. Today the ideological power is consumerism. The Roman Empire encompassed sixty to sixty-five million people from Britain to northern Africa, and ruled by co-opting local elites. The United States, with 4 percent of the world's population, rules in a similar way. The American Empire extends around the globe through political understandings whereby foreign nations grant the United States control in international affairs in exchange for recognition of their own internal affairs, whether they be democracies such as Italy or dictatorships such as Kuwait. Roman legions, stationed across the empire, established peace through warfare and victory. Over five thousand American military bases in the United States, its territories, and at least thirty-eight other countries maintain American global control. Rome's economic base was tributes, taxes, and rent from conquered peoples. American economic power resides in control of 34 percent of all global wealth.[4] In the Gospel of Mark, a man "with many possessions" asked Jesus what he must do to enter the realm of God. Many of us ask the same question today.

We ask and see from where we stand. I am a white, middle-class, educated, heterosexual woman who has worked in social welfare and public health, principally in maternal and child health, for almost fifty years. I recognize the particular subordination and vulnerability of women across generations and empires. As Otto Maduro writes, "the majority of the poor are women; the majority of women are poor; and the poorest of the poor are women."[5] It has always been so. Not surprisingly, women were Jesus' most faithful followers, following him to the cross and the empty tomb. To them the messenger at the tomb declared that Jesus had risen and gone ahead to Galilee, where those who sought him would see him. Mark gives us enough clues to believe that women were pivotal in Jesus' ministry and in the movement that followed his crucifixion. Study of the New Testament and early Christian writings has led feminist scholars to conclude that Jesus' ministry during his lifetime was a Jewish "discipleship of equals."[6] To promote that discipleship today, I have brought women into the forefront in these reflections.

I remember one woman who epitomizes for me empowerment and liberation; we met outside a Coptic Orthodox clinic in southern Egypt. In the desert sands to the north and south along the Nile lay ruins of Christian monasteries dating to the fourth century. It was ancient Christian land that had produced saints who gave witness in the formation of the church and martyrs who died in the Roman persecution of Christians. On the walls of Pharaonic temples were graffiti scratched by Roman legionnaires while Jesus healed in Roman-occupied Galilee, as well as later graffiti claiming the space for Christian worship, as Jesus' followers took up his command to proclaim the good news to the whole world. Now the region is predominantly Muslim; the Coptic Church is embattled, and mission programs are empowered by foreign mission giving.

A woman dressed in black robes (a *burka*) from head to toe rushed up to me and grabbed my hand. Gesturing between us, she said, "same." She pointed to her eyes, just visible through the grilled eye slits in her *burka*, and to mine. We were blue-eyed in a Nubian region of dark eyes. She threw back her head wrap to reveal a white face and red hair. She smiled and said again, "same." Through translators she told me of her life. At twelve she had been given as a second wife to a Nubian farmer as payment for her father's debts. Her first child was born a year later. She had eighteen pregnancies; ten children lived past childhood. That day, she was accompanying a granddaughter for family planning after the birth of a third child. She declared her granddaughter would be able to have a better life than she had; she could make choices. She would not watch helplessly as child after child died. This mission clinic empowered the most vulnerable, and I could hear "hallelujahs" rise from the ancient ruins along the river, in this region so formative in early Christianity and now dependent on wider Christian discipleship for mission support.

In our journey, we walk with disciples across two thousand years around the globe. Following my 1977 encounter at the Indian pond, I volunteered as a United Church of Christ (UCC) mission exchange person from Rhode Island to the Jaffna Diocese of the Church of South India in Sri Lanka. Staying at the Udivil Girls College, founded by nineteenth-century New England Congregational missionaries in the north of Sri Lanka, I experienced the church in the Two-Thirds World and returned to the United States two months later torn between seminary and direct action for justice and development. Choosing the latter and working for secular nonprofit health, social welfare, and development agencies for over thirty years in thirty-five countries of the Two-Thirds World of Latin America, Africa, the Middle East, and Asia, I also encountered the church in direct action for justice and peace in country after country from Latin America to Africa, the Middle East and Asia.

In these reflections on the Gospel of Mark, I have tried to give a face and a voice to that Two-Thirds World I have known, and to identify modern disciples I have encountered. Such disciples, both famous and relatively unknown, give us hope that, as Dr. Martin Luther King, Jr., frequently said, quoting the nineteenth-century abolitionist minister Theodore Parker, "The arc of the moral universe is long, but it bends toward justice." Some disciples worked in Coptic clinics in ancient Christian lands. Some ran clinics for victims of domestic violence and rape in a Kenyan refugee camp plagued by violence, scarcity, and trauma. Some served in American soup lines; others funded food distribution in camps for Somali refugees along the Kenyan border. Some protested outside the White House; others held prayer vigils in their churches. Some volunteer in hospices; others are recipients of hospice care. Some, like Dr. Martin Luther King, Jr., and Archbishop Oscar Romero, gave their lives for the disenfranchised, justice, and their faith. The reflections begin in the Roman Empire and pass through Washington, DC, Rhode Island, and Angola. The journey to Galilee, where Mark's Jesus said he would meet us, lies open on roads across the globe.

CHAPTER 1

EMPIRE IN
FIRST-CENTURY PALESTINE _____

The Roman Empire

The Gospel of Mark, the good news of Jesus the Messiah, was written within the Roman Empire almost two thousand years ago. During Jesus' life and the later composition of Mark, the empire stretched from Britain to Spain, to Turkey and south to Egypt. Rome seized this vast territory, nation by nation and people by people, through military power. It extracted the labor, produce, and wealth of the people through economic power, backed by the military. It controlled political power and the way the society was organized by co-opting each nation's elites. In these lands of many gods, it sought to maintain ideological power over the people through an ideology and mystification of the Roman emperor Caesar as god.

Empire is a "form of political organization in which the social elements that rule in the dominant state . . . create a network of allied elites in regions abroad who accept subordination in international affairs in return for security of their position" in their own country.[1] Empire includes four interdependent types of power: "military power, the monopoly or control of force and violence; economic power, the monopoly or control of labor and production; political power, the monopoly or control of organization and institution; and ideological power, the monopoly or control of meaning and interpretation."[2] Bureaucracy holds empire together and maintains patterns of privilege, poverty, and stabilized inequality.

Roman Military Power: Peace through Victory

Rome conquered this expanse of territory through its legions, highly trained men who traveled and fought with swords with which to kill and shovels with which to build roads. Although we in recent centuries have glorified the Roman Empire, admiring the beauty of its art and the genius of its architecture, for the conquered of the empire, including Jesus' Palestine, life was often miserable. One Roman historian, depicting Roman conquest through the eyes of the conquered, wrote: "Robbers of the world, now that earth fails their all-devastating hands, they probe even the sea: if their enemy have wealth, they have greed; if he be poor, they are ambitious; East nor West has glutted them; alone of mankind they covet with the same passion want [poor lands] as much as wealth [rich lands]. To plunder, butcher, steal, these things they misname empire: they make desolation and they call it peace."[3]

Roman Political Power: Subjugation, Then Rule through Local Elites

Rome usually ruled through a three-step process. First was military conquest by the legions. It was a brutal conquest without mercy for women, men, or children. Resistance was met with torturous death, such as crucifixion, which was meant to terrorize the population into submission. When terror had sufficiently subdued the people, Rome worked to co-opt local elites. Once effective organized opposition had been eliminated, "with a limited exercise of intelligence," force could be "transformed into authority and might into right."[4]

Accommodating local elites, who benefited from Roman roads, public baths, and civic honors, served as Rome's public face, legitimizing the "right" of acquiescence to Caesar. However, behind the appearance of local rule lay Roman power, which replaced the elites if they did not toe the line, and the legions, which moved quickly to suppress rebellion. Some nations in Hellenistic Asia Minor, where the Apostle Paul would later preach, slid relatively easily into the Roman Empire. Other nations such as Palestine fought the empire and its exploitation.

Roman Economic Power: Enforced Tribute

In the advanced agrarian societies of the Roman Empire, the elites were a tiny percentage of the population. The vast majority were peasant farming families who eked out a living on small family holdings or who had lost their land and become sharecroppers or day laborers. Rome built its wealth through enforced tribute upon the production of such farms throughout the empire. From Palestine, Rome extracted olive oil and grapes. From Egypt and Sicily came tribute corn for the dole to Rome's urban masses. From northern Africa came grain and olive oil; this triumphal arch to the emperor at the gates to the city of Volubilis (modern Morocco), overlooking those conquered fertile plains, celebrated the empire (Illus. 1.1). Throughout the empire, men, women, and children, in a resulting downward spiral of poverty and debt, became indentured or sold themselves into slavery. Jesus' parables speak to this context.

Ideological Power: Worship of Caesar as God and Savior

Roman imperial theology—the worship of the Roman emperor (Caesar) as god—began with the deification of Julius Caesar after his assassination in 44 B.C.E. Each Caesar thereafter assumed "divinity" or was recognized as divine. Caesar Augustus (63 B.C.E.–14 C.E.), who ended the Roman civil war that erupted after Julius Caesar's death and ruled during the time of Jesus' birth, was worshipped as the "Son of God," the "Savior," and "Father of His Country." The Roman god Apollo was proclaimed to be his father.

1.1 Roman triumphal arch at Volubis

1.2 Roman temple to Caesar Augustus

Historian Richard Horsley writes, "Roman imperial theology" should be "understood not as propaganda from imperial top to colonial bottom but as an extremely successful advertising campaign supported by self-consciously 'Roman' political elites across the entire empire."[5] Elites, ever eager to move up the ladder of patronage, vied with one another to honor Caesar in grand ways. Temples in which Caesar was worshipped and monuments to Caesar were important ways to gain status.

This temple to Caesar Augustus (Illus. 1.2), built on a hill outside modern Ankara, Turkey (ancient Asia Minor), honors him with walls inscribed in Greek and Latin with the *Res gestae divi Augusti* (*The Achievements of the Divine Augustus*) that Augustus wrote to eulogize himself. For me, tracing the footsteps of the Apostle Paul who would proclaim "Christ crucified" in the heart of the Roman Empire less than fifty years after this temple was erected and before Mark was written, it was a stunning view of the ideological battle between Jesus and Caesar. In his own eulogy, Augustus boasts of his conquests, the countries conquered, the kings and their children who were forced to march as captives before his chariot, and the slaves recaptured. Caesar was named "savior" and "son of God"; Jesus will be given the same titles in the Gospel of Mark. What different saviors they are! Caesar lauded himself as follows:

> I undertook many civil and foreign wars by land and sea through-out the world. . . . When foreign peoples could safely be pardoned I preferred to preserve rather than to exterminate them. . . . In my triumphs nine kings or children of kings were led before my chariot. . . . I gave three gladiatorial games . . . at these games some 10,000 men took part in combat. . . . I produced a naval battle as a show for the people. . . . About 3,000 men, besides the rowers, fought in these fleets. . . . I captured about 30,000 slaves who had escaped from their masters and taken up arms against the republic, and I handed them over to their masters for punish-ment. . . . I extended the territory of all those provinces of the Roman people on whose borders lay peoples not subject to our government.[6]

In every region, on-duty Roman troops or colonizing ex-Roman sol-diers and Roman culture exerted their power. Everywhere, Rome established its culture and commerce. Imposition of Roman currency and monetization of local economies were means of control and ways to share Roman imperial theology. Roman coins have been found from Scotland to Afghanistan.

In 63 B.C.E. Rome conquered Palestine and established a Jewish client king, Herod ("Herod the Great"), as "King of the Jews" follow-ing a period of civil war. With the death of Herod in 4 B.C.E., Rome divided the rule of Palestine among his three sons: Herod Antipas in Galilee, Archelaus in Judea and Samaria, and Herod Philip in north-eastern Palestine. Each of these Herodian (of Herod's family) rulers was a client of Rome and ruled at Rome's behest. In 6 C.E., with the death of Archelaus, Rome stationed its own commander in Jerusalem who ruled Judea and Samaria through the priestly aristocracy of the Jewish temple-state in Jerusalem.

CHAPTER 2

PALESTINE
IN THE FIRST CENTURY _____

Geography

Jesus of Nazareth was a Jew, and all his early followers were Jews in Palestine, the most rebellious of Rome's conquered territories, a land in monotheist covenant with one God, Yahweh. The region, lying between the Assyrian/Babylonian Empires to the east and Egypt to the southwest, had been a battleground for the previous thousand years, as indigenous Canaanite tribes and foreign empires warred over the land. Greeks, Romans, and Jewish elites lived in cities while the Jewish peasantry lived in villages and the countryside. Through it and into the neighboring gentile areas, Jesus crossed borders: in Galilee, north into the Phoenician region of Tyre and Sidon, across the Sea of Galilee into the Decapolis ("ten cities" in Greek), through Samaria and to Jerusalem in Judea. Galilee, through which Jesus crisscrossed on his ministry of healing and exorcisms in the first half of Mark, was a region of fertile rolling hills and valleys with small-scale farming and estates owned by absentee landlords. Around the Sea of Galilee, where Jesus called his disciples, were rich soil and developed fisheries that prepared salted fish for export. Upper Galilee was more rugged, a maze of higher hills, valleys, gorges, and peaks, and the site of imperial granaries storing tribute grain for Rome.[1]

Although Jesus was a border crosser in geographic and social terms, all four Gospels indicate he avoided the two major Galilean cities, Tiberias and Sepphoris, which were established by Herod Antipas. Both were centers of Herodian power and exploitation, inhabited by Herodian allies and elites. Tiberias, along the Lake of Galilee, was named in honor of Emperor Tiberius. Previously, Antipas had rebuilt Sepphoris, the capital of Galilee, on the crossroads of two Roman

11

roads, only a few miles from Nazareth, Jesus' birthplace. Destroyed by the Romans after it revolted in 4 B.C.E., Sepphoris was rebuilt and fortified to be "the ornament of all Galilee" and the center from which the Romans ruled and taxed Galilee with the cooperation of the collaborating Jewish aristocracy. Sean Freyne describes these cities as "alien to and parasitical on the surrounding territory" and complicit in rural impoverishment. "An urban culture introduced new types into the population . . . acting on behalf of the ruling elite and the native aristocracy. It also made new demands for goods and services—thereby, however, increasing the burden of taxation on the peasantry. This pressure from the top inevitably led to an increase in poverty, and the slide from landowner to tenant farmer to day labourers, to beggars, all characters we hear of in Jesus' parables, was inexorable."[2]

Jesus' ministry was in the impoverished countryside. Across the border from Galilee in Phoenicia, crowds received Jesus in rural areas outside the city of Tyre, where three cultures, Hellenistic, Jewish, and Phoenician, met.[3] Like Sepphoris, Tyre was a rich city that depended on the countryside for food; in the struggle for food between Tyre and the countryside, the countryside always lost. Gerd Theissen quotes the second-century Roman philosopher Galen on the resulting famines:

> The city people, who, as is customary, store up enough food in summer to last the whole year, take all the wheat from the fields together with the barley, beans and lentils, and leave the country people nothing but the remaining pulses, although they themselves even take the greater part of that, too, into the cities. The country people then, when they have used up their winter supplies, have only unhealthy nourishment through the entire summer. In that period these country people eat the shoots and suckers of unhealthful plants.[4]

The hinterland of Tyre and the struggle between the urban elite and the rural poor provided the context for Mark's story of the foreign woman who sought healing for her daughter. Healing, disease, and illness are central in the Gospel because malnutrition, infectious and contagious diseases, unclean water, accidents, war, and early and frequent childbearing led to illness and early death. For good reason, healings are important in the Gospel. Girls normally married at puberty or as early as age twelve and began childbearing thereafter; such early child-bearing would have been an important factor in low life expectancy for the average person, estimated at twenty-five years.[5]

Mark sets many of the healing and miracle stories across the river Jordan in the Decapolis, a region with a mixed population, Hellenistic cities, and Roman legions. Here, Jesus drives out "Legion," walks on water, heals the deaf and mute man, and feeds the four thousand. On a road outside Caesarea Philippi, the city built in Caesar's honor, Peter recognizes Jesus as Christ. Throughout the first ten chapters of Mark, religious leaders come from Jerusalem in Judea to watch Jesus and his disciples. From chapter 11 to the end, Jesus is in Judea, the heart of Judaism, where the focus is on Jerusalem, Jesus' confrontation with the temple and Roman authorities, his final witness and nonviolent resistance, the crucifixion, and the empty tomb.

Israelite Tradition: The Great Tradition and the Little Tradition

Six to seven hundred years before Jesus was born, Jewish scholars began formally collecting, developing, and writing a theological "interpretation" of the Israelite people and their understanding of their God, Yahweh.[6] The people had known conquest, oppression, massacre, exile, and return. But through it all, the tradition and experience of God as the faithful, righteous one who hears the cries of the people and liberates them lived on. It was time to celebrate, remember, consolidate the people, and forge communal identity anew. The oral stories and traditions from ancient Israel and from Babylon were woven together with priestly writings and liturgies to tell the story of God's steadfast love, justice, and righteousness.

With the beginning of the Exodus story, when God heard the cry of God's people and led them to freedom, the Lord was a faithful God. From the beginning of their relationship with the Lord, God responded with "the passion of holy power" to the Israelites' "human cry."[7]

> Then the Lord said, "I have observed the misery of my people who are in Egypt; I have heard their cry on account of their taskmasters. Indeed, I know their sufferings, and I have come down to deliver them from the Egyptians, and to bring them up out of that land to a good and broad land, a land flowing with milk and

honey. . . . The cry of the Israelites has now come to me; I have also seen how the Egyptians oppress them." (Exod. 3:7-9)

In the Exodus story, Yahweh pledged to be Israel's God, and they committed to be God's people, living by the instruction given to Moses on Sinai (Exod. 19:1-6). As the written Torah was developed over the centuries and the witness and prophecy of the prophets were added, God consistently commanded justice and righteousness. From the Sinai covenant to the cries of the later prophets, God condemned exploitation of the alien, the widow, and the orphan, groups who were synonymous with vulnerability and poverty.

> If you lend money to my people, to the poor among you, you shall not deal with them as a creditor; you shall not exact interest from them. If you take your neighbor's cloak in pawn, you shall restore it before the sun goes down; for it may be your neighbor's only clothing to use as cover; in what else shall that person sleep? And if your neighbor cries out to me, I will listen, for I am compassionate. (Exod. 22:25-27)

> When you reap the harvest of your land, you shall not reap to the very edges of your field, or gather the gleanings of your harvest; you shall leave them for the poor and for the alien: I am the Lord your God. (Lev. 23:22)

> Thus says the Lord: Act with justice and righteousness, and deliver from the hand of the oppressor anyone who has been robbed. And do no wrong or violence to the alien, the orphan, and the widow, nor shed innocent blood in this place. (Jer. 22:3)

By the time of Jesus' birth, the scriptures that comprise the modern Hebrew Bible, the Torah, the Prophets, and the Writings (including the Psalms), were completed, translated from the Hebrew into other languages, and existed on precious scrolls in synagogues throughout the empire. "People studied scripture, memorized it, and tried to live by it. In order to understand God's ways, they meditated upon it. When praying, they quoted from it liberally, and in their public liturgies they read it and studied it."[8] Additionally, other important Israelite "texts about God and Israel" that did not make the Hebrew canon were influential during the first century. These texts, called Pseudepigrapha by scholars and written in the first centuries before and after Jesus' birth, bridge the scriptures in the Hebrew and Christian canons: "many are apocalyptic visions or heavenly tours that purported to offer a God's eye perspective on current events." The texts of the book of Daniel (included in the Christian canon but not the Hebrew), the *Parables of 1 Enoch*, and the *Psalms of Solomon* were important for Mark's Jesus.[9]

The first century in Palestine was a time of rebellion, renewal, and intra-Judaism debate: a people seeking to realize the realm of God in the face of Roman occupation and exploitation. Jesus and other Jews in other movements sought to renew Israel from their different understandings of the Torah, temple, and idolatrous collusion with Rome. Above the temple gate hung a giant imperial eagle, symbol of Roman control over the Jewish temple, a grandiose structure expanded by Herod the Great after Rome installed him as "King of the Jews."[10] In the temple, in subservience to Rome and contrary to prohibitions against idolatry, the priests offered sacrifices to Caesar and to Rome as well as to Yahweh.

The temple-state was the political, economic, and ideological center of Palestine. Richard Horsley describes it as "the guardian of the great tradition" through which the rulers defined and propagated their definition of reality through their interpretation of the Torah.

> Through the media of inspired texts and sacred scriptures, the great tradition defines what is real and identifies that reality with the current social, political, and economic order. Clearly, the carrier of that great tradition in first-century Palestine was the Torah, and the group that could control the interpretation of the Torah could define "world," that social and political construction of reality that could specify the meaning of purity, demand tithes, and control behavior. The great tradition is usually grounded in an urban center and, in Jesus' time, that center was Jerusalem.[11]

There was no separation of politics and religion. The temple-state was a religious, economic, and political institution all in one. Taxes flowed into the temple from Jewish communities throughout Palestine and the Diaspora; the descendants of the former ruling groups of Israel had rebuilt the temple after the exile and ensured its financial security through a series of tithes.[12] New Testament scholar William Herzog II writes, "The temple was, therefore, at the very heart of the system of economic exploitation made possible by the monetizing of the economy and the concentration of wealth made possible by investing the temple and its leaders with the powers and rewards of a collaborating aristocracy."[13] A large proportion of each peasant family's yield was annually demanded in tithes and dues by the temple to support its functions and priests.[14] "It was no accident that one of the first acts of the First Jewish Revolt in 66 C.E. was the burning of the debt records in the archives in Jerusalem."[15]

New scholarship on tumultuous first-century Judaism in the context of Roman occupation has led to new understandings of the century's religious diversity and debate. It has also led to better understanding of three groups identified in the Gospels as monitoring and challenging Jesus: the scribes, the Pharisees, and the Sadducees. The scribes were retainers working for the temple-state or government in some form, and the Pharisees were most likely some sort of association or "political-interest group" among such retainers. The Sadducees were a lay aristocratic group of power brokers. In monitoring Jesus, they all acted on behalf of Jewish elites under the control of Rome and the temple-state.

The ritualized purity and debt codes came out of the temple-state and Great Tradition and, as presented in Mark, were monitored by the Pharisees and scribes. Jesus' noncompliance with these codes is a frequent source of conflict, as it would have been for other Jews struggling with holiness in that context. Ched Myers writes that the codes had originated as group boundaries to maintain Israel as a holy people, but had come to stratify the people, reinforce class boundaries, and exclude the poor. Peasants working in the fields could not afford the time or the money to establish or maintain ritual purity. Pollution came from contact with daily or regular bodily fluids: "semen, urine, spittle, blood."[16]

In contrast to the Great Tradition centered in Jerusalem was the Little Tradition, centered in the peasant countryside. Herzog writes,

> Needless to say, peasants take a dim view of the great tradition, although they do not have enough power to oppose it directly. This leads to the formation of a "shadow society," that is, a "pattern of structural, stylistic and normative opposition to the polit-

ico-religious tradition of ruling elites." The ideological task of the rulers is to transfer their view of the great tradition to their peasant masses and implant it in their villages. The peasants' task is to resist domination implied in the project.[17]

Supporting the peasants' resistance were scripture, oral stories, and the dissident memory of their God who responded with "the passion of holy power" to "human cry." The "Exodus-Sinai memory" of a God who passionately acted for justice and righteousness had produced "an uncommon social ethic" among the people. The synagogue scrolls documented it in numerous ways:

- Debts owed by the poor are to be canceled after seven years, so that there is no permanent underclass (Deut. 15:1-18): "remember that you were a slave in the land of Egypt, and the Lord your God redeemed you" (v. 15).
- No interest is to be charged on loans to members of the community (Deut. 23:19-20).
- Permanent hospitality is to be extended to runaway slaves (Deut. 23:15-16).
- No collateral is to be required on loans made to poor people (Deut. 24:10-13).
- No withholding of wages that are due to the poor (Deut. 24:14-15).
- No injustice toward a resident alien or an orphan (Deut. 24:17-18).[18]

Supporting the "Exodus-Sinai memory" were the prophets' insistent challenges to the rich that society cease its worship of idols; return to worship the one God, Yahweh; and care for the poor, widowed, and orphaned. In the eighth century B.C.E., Hosea had critiqued the monarchy for trusting in its power and foreign alliances rather than in God and the Sinai covenant.[19] In such prophetic challenges, as Old Testament theologian Walter Brueggemann writes, the critiqued worship of "false gods is never separate from the socioeconomic charge of practicing injustice."[20] Sinning in the following text is being unfaithful to God's commandments for righteousness, justice, and mercy.

And now they keep on sinning and make a cast image for them-selves, idols of silver made according to their understanding, all of them the work of artisans. "Sacrifice to these," they say. People are kissing calves! Therefore they shall be like the morning mist or like the dew that goes away early, like chaff that swirls from the threshing-floor or like smoke from a window. Yet I have been the Lord your God ever since the land of Egypt; you know no God but me, and besides me there is no savior. It was I who fed you in the wilderness, in the land of drought. When I fed them, they were satisfied; they were satisfied, and their heart was proud; therefore they forgot me. (Hos. 13:2-6)

On the synagogue scrolls, the prophets said that for the people's idolatry, the northern kingdom of Israel had fallen to the Assyrians and the southern kingdom to the Babylonians. Isaiah and Micah, prophets preaching justice and righteousness to the powerful during those years, served as an inspiration for Mark's Jesus hundreds of years later.[21]

Is not this the fast that I choose: to loose the bonds of injustice, to undo the thongs of the yoke, to let the oppressed go free, and to break every yoke? Is it not to share your bread with the hun-gry, and bring the homeless poor into your house; when you see the naked, to cover them, and not to hide yourself from your own kin? Then your light shall break forth like the dawn, and your healing shall spring up quickly; your vindicator shall go before you, the glory of the Lord shall be your rearguard. Then you shall call, and the Lord will answer; you shall cry for help, and he will say, Here I am. (Isa. 58:3-9)

"With what shall I come before the Lord, and bow myself before God on high? Shall I come before him with burnt-offerings, with calves a year old? Will the Lord be pleased with thousands of rams, with tens of thousands of rivers of oil? Shall I give my first-born for my transgression, the fruit of my body for the sin of my soul?" He has told you, O mortal, what is good; and what does the Lord require of you but to do justice, and to love kindness, and to walk humbly with your God? (Mic. 6:6-8)

The Lord rises to argue his case; he stands to judge the peoples. The Lord enters into judgment with the elders and princes of his people: It is you who have devoured the vineyard; the spoil of the poor is in your houses. What do you mean by crushing my people, by grinding the face of the poor? says the Lord God of hosts. (Isa. 3:13-15)

Socio-Economic Desperation under Occupation

Palestine was a traditional advanced agrarian society, that is, it was a society based on land and agriculture that was ruled by elites who comprised only 1 to 2 percent of society. The wealth of the elites was due to their control of the land and of the peasants who were forced to yield any surplus, through tribute, tithes, and rent, to their masters. Rome, like previous empires, believed it owned both the land and the peoples living upon it. In good times, peasants subsisted; in bad times they starved due to a triple "taxation": dues and tithes to the temple, Roman tribute, and, in Galilee, tribute to the urban aristocracy.

Traditionally, this enforced payment of crops, labor, and cash has been called "taxation"; however, in reality, the word is inappropriate in this context, because it connotes an exchange of benefits. First-century Palestinian peasants received nothing from Rome or the Herodian cities in exchange for the mandated payments to the powerful, which Herzog estimates amounted to 20 to 35 percent of a subsistence family's production.[22] Additionally, Rome drained the peasant economy with special "taxes" for its wars and with devastation wrought in the countryside in battles to subdue the population. Peasants steadily lost their land. Many became sharecroppers on land previously theirs for generations but now owned by absentee landlords; others became day laborers, an even more precarious existence.

Jesus' ministry occurs in this context of exploitation and misery, framed by the promises of God. Yahweh, a God of justice, had given the land to Israel in covenant, to be divided and shared among the twelve tribes. To protect the poor and to ensure debt was not passed on generation after generation, there was to be a sabbatical year every seventh year. Some crops were to be left in the fields, some grapes on the vine, and some olives on the trees so that the poor might glean and even the wild animals might eat (Exod. 23:10-11).

Roman Domination and Palestinian Resistance

Palestinians did not quietly submit. If God had given Israel the land, how could a ruling class presume they had the right to take it from the people? Traditional memories of the God who led the Jewish people out of slavery to freedom under Moses' leadership did not die. Hope and the conviction that the people were called to worship one God, and only one God, did not die. The knowledge that their God demanded justice and mercy for the vulnerable lived on and nourished resistance, both hidden and overt. Horsley, building on the work of James C. Scott, writes that "all forms of protest and resistance, hidden or overt, are rooted in what has been called the 'hidden transcript' of the subject people." This "hidden transcript" is distinct from the "public transcript" and results from "the conflictual dynamics of power relations between the dominant elite and the people subordinated to them."

> Much of the behavior and speech of slaves, peasants and workers is coerced. The open interaction and communication between the powerful and subordinated . . . is determined by elites. Thus most of our written sources, which represent this "official transcript," tell only part of the historical story of power relations, from the viewpoint of the powerful. However, every subordinate group creates, out of its ordeal, a "hidden transcript" that represents a critique of power spoken behind the back of the dominant, in sequestered sites.[23]

The hidden transcript of first-century Israelites held the Exodus-Sinai tradition, the prophets' calls for justice and righteousness, and Isaiah's vision of a new Jerusalem (Isaiah 65:17-25). Pseudepigraphal texts were part of that hidden transcript, continuing the prophetic critique and nurturing resistance. Wes Howard-Brook identifies the following passages from the *Parables of 1 Enoch*, written probably during Jesus' lifetime, as one such resistance text.[24] In it the author equated "'sin' with imperial oppression" and then proclaimed a "Son of Man" who would enable righteousness and be a light to the nations.[25]

> When [the Lord of Spirits'] hidden things are revealed to the righteous, the sinners will be judged, and the wicked will be

driven from the presence of the righteous and chosen. And thereafter, it will not be the mighty and exalted who possess the earth. . . . (38:3-4a)

And then the kings and the mighty will perish, and they will be given into the hand of the righteous and holy, and from then on, no one will seek mercy for them from the Lord of Spirits, for their life will be at an end. (38:5-6)

He will be a staff for the righteous, that they may lean on him and not fall; and he will be the light of the nations, and he will be a hope for those who grieve in their hearts. All who dwell on the earth will fall down and worship before him, and they will glorify and bless and sing hymns to the name of the Lord of Spirits. (48:4-5)

He has preserved the portion of the righteous, for they have hated and despised this age of unrighteousness; indeed, all its deeds and its ways they have hated in the name of the Lord of Spirits. For in his name they are saved, and he is the vindicator of their lives. (48:7)

The hidden transcript was the theological basis for protest, civil disobedience and rebellion, and Palestinians resisted from the beginning of the conquest in 63 B.C.E. until their devastating defeat following the Bar Kokhba revolt of 132–136 C.E. An early act of civil disobedience took place soon after the Roman conquest in 63 B.C.E., when two Torah scholars in the temple led forty students in tearing down the Roman eagle over the temple gate; the Romans responded by burning alive the scholars and students. But resistance continued, in forms Horsley calls "popular prophetic and messianic movements."[26] Ten years later, Judas the Galilean led a revolt against new Roman taxation. Twenty years later, Jesus of Nazareth, working at the village level as a "shadow society and an alternative moral universe," continued the resistance against idolatry, brokenness, and exploitation.[27]

From the beginning, Rome responded brutally to resistance in ways that would have collectively traumatized the people, including those later involved in the Jesus movement.[28] Ten years after their initial conquest, to put down a civil war between rival factions of the government

Rome had installed, Roman troops enslaved thirty thousand people in and around Magdala on the Sea of Galilee. Fifty years later, about the time of Jesus' birth, in retaliation for rebellion, Roman troops burned the town of Sepphoris, enslaved men, women, and children, and crucified about two thousand people. Sepphoris was only four miles across a valley from Nazareth, Jesus' hometown. Following the revolt, his family and neighbors could have seen the Roman roads lined with the corpses of crucified men and weeping women and children. In addition, over the years, countless men, women, and children were taken into Roman slavery.

After Jesus' crucifixion, resistance continued. Confronted with the prospect of a statue of Emperor Caligula in the temple, Galilean peasants struck, threatening agricultural revenues and tribute to Rome. Caligula responded by sending two legions from Syria; the potential revolt ended with the death of Caligula as the legions assembled on the coast and prepared to march inland. From 66 to 73 C.E., the Jewish people rebelled against Rome. In 70 C.E., Jerusalem fell to the Roman legions after a prolonged siege of the city, during which time the Jews fought among themselves, residents died of starvation and disease, and Rome daily crucified so many men outside the city walls that there was hardly room for all the crosses. When the city finally fell, there were mass crucifixions, enslavement, flight, and exile of Judean Jews.

Most scholars presume the Gospel of Mark was written during this four-year period of rebellion, chaos, and despair. Behind it lay forty years of oral history of Jesus' ministry. As Jesus preached, healed, and confronted the poverty, oppression, and brokenness of the Jewish people, those healed, comforted, and astounded by his ministry remembered and relayed to others stories and sayings of this man who had given them and their communities a way to wholeness and new life. After the crucifixion, these memories and new patterns of discipleship lived on and were passed on, from community to community and from Palestine to neighboring nations. In time, during the Roman suppression of occupied Palestine, Mark wove the stories of resistance, love, and hope into the narrative we know as the Gospel of Mark. The message of Mark is discipleship, liberation, and new life.

We do not know the Gospel's author or where it was written. Scholars follow the tradition of referring to the author as "Mark," though the actual name and gender of the author are unknown. In the second century, the tradition grew up of connecting the unnamed author with the name "Mark," perhaps the "John Mark" mentioned in Luke's Acts of the Apostles.[29]

CHAPTER 3

Empire Today _____

The sole superpower in a globally interdependent world, the United States has powers similar to those of the Roman Empire during Jesus' ministry and at the time of the writing of the Gospel of Mark. It is the interactive, interdependent combination of these powers—ideological power, economic power, political power, and military power—that makes for empire today as it did two thousand years ago. Roman roads cut through mountains, bridged rivers, and crossed deserts, enabling conquest, and opening communication and trade. Legions were stationed from Britain to Syria within striking distance of conquered lands. Statues of Caesar filled the empire. African grain fed the people of Rome. Sometimes, grace also passed along those routes: stories of Jesus from community to community, Galilee to Asia Minor, and to Rome itself.

Today, we are tied together in similar ways, magnified by globalization, the ideological, economic, political, cultural, and technological aspects of which permeate the globe. While sitting in clothes made in Bangladesh and Honduras, we in New England drink coffee from Kenya and eat fruit from Mexico on cups and plates made in China, worry about urban unemployment, and watch television news of floods leaving hundreds of thousands homeless in Pakistan. Oil to heat our homes and to fuel planes for global transport of food comes from the Middle and Near East, convulsed in turmoil and nationalist fervor. Simultaneously throughout the Two-Thirds World, in small villages lit by several lone electrical poles, teens crowd Internet "cafes" for visions of the fantastic life of the First World, where water comes from a faucet, everyone owns a refrigerator, stores are filled with food, and the good life is portrayed as available to all. Catholic, Protestant, Orthodox, Jew, and other, we contribute to relief and development efforts in Haiti following the 2009 earthquake; a year later, we pray for the thirty-three miners trapped in the collapsed gold mine two thousand feet below the surface of the Chilean desert. Grace passes along the modern routes of empire too.

Ideological Power: Consumerism

The Roman Empire was built on imperial theology; Rome co-opted elites with the promise of safety and success if they were obedient to the empire and worship of Caesar. Today, American society and American Empire are built upon consumerism, and most people put their faith in acquiring material things and material success. Many believe we are defined by what we consume. We mistake prosperity and the abundance of things for God's blessings; we mistake personal material wealth—even a nation's or a church's material wealth—for divine approval. We are taught to consume as a toddler in front of the television, and consume we do into old age, in an ever-expanding mirage of material wants and needs. Things that were unknown or luxuries thirty years ago have become the norm: think of air conditioning, computers, color televisions, and cell phones. While 40 percent of the world's people do not have access to even a simple pit latrine and 20 percent have no safe drinking water, the standard of living of average American adults has risen over the standards of their parents. While American family size has declined over the last fifty years, the size of homes has doubled.

Despite the Great Recession's devastating effects on the middle class and the poor, the ideological power of consumerism holds the American people in thrall. New economies spring up, claiming to meet new needs. A simple example, close to home for many of us, is the pet economy. In 2007 Americans spent $41 billion on their pets—more than the gross domestic products of all but sixty-four countries in the world. *Businessweek* described the phenomenon:

> The rising status of pets has started an unprecedented wave of entrepreneurship in an industry once epitomized by felt mice and rubber balls. There are now $430 indoor potties, $30-an-ounce perfume, and $225 trench coats aimed solely at four-footed consumers and their wallet-toting companions. Even those who shun animal couture are increasingly willing to spend thousands on drugs for depression . . . in pets, as well as . . . end-of-life care.[1]

During the 2010 Christmas season, as parts of the country pulled out of the Great Recession, *Consumer Reports* revealed that 26 percent of those polled planned to give their pets a gift for the holiday season.[2]

At the end of the year, online holiday shopping totals had "surpassed the levels of the past few years to set a new record for spending at almost $31 billion." The National Mail Order Association wrote that holiday shopping had returned to a state that could "only be described as a very merry holiday shopping season."[3] As Christians in the American Empire, how do we understand such a Christmas season in a world where billions of humans have little to eat and little to wear, let alone health care?

Economic Power: A World of "Haves and Have-Nots"

We live in a world of "haves and have-nots," with shocking disparities of well-being within the United States and between those in the First World and those in the Two-Thirds World. A recent study reveals that the richest 2 percent of adults own more than half of all the household wealth in the world; the richest 10 percent of adults in the world own 85 percent of global household wealth! The United States and Canada, with 5 percent of the globe's population, own 34 percent of all global wealth.[4]

Visions of American affluence stream across the globe, attracting migrants from around the world. Yet reality is more complex and painful than we, stratified by race, class, and gender, often acknowledge. Although over the last fifty years the percentage of Americans living in poverty has declined, the number of Americans living in poverty in 2010—46.2 million—is the largest number since the government began to publish such data fifty-two years ago. It was the third annual consecutive increase in the poverty rate.[5]

For the last twenty years in the United States, the rich have gotten richer and the poor have gotten poorer, in terms of both wealth and income. Income is the money a person receives from employment, interest, rents, and transfers from others; wealth is the value of all assets, including real estate, money, stocks, pensions, and cars. The median household income is highest for those who are married, for men, and for whites. From 1997 to 2000, the net wealth of the wealthiest families soared; the median wealth of the top 10 percent of families increased from $492,400 in 1997 to $833,600 in 2000.[6] The following table presents a stunning picture of wealth in the United States in 2001; the distribution has become even more skewed since then because of the Great Recession. The poorest 30 percent of American households were in debt, their debts exceeded their assets, or they had nothing and owed nothing. The wealthiest 10 percent of American households held 70 percent of American wealth.[7]

Distribution of American Wealth, 2001

	Share of Lowest									Share of Top		
Percent of American households	10%	20%	30%	40%	50%	60%	70%	80%	90%	10%	5%	1%
Percent of wealth	0%	0%	0%	1%	3%	6%	10%	17%	30%	70%	58%	33%

There are major disparities by race, ethnicity, gender, and marital status in income and wealth. American racial and ethnic differences are now the largest since the government began publishing such data a quarter century ago and are roughly twice the size of ratios that had prevailed between whites, blacks, and Hispanics for the twenty years prior to the Great Recession, which ended in 2009.[8] In 2009 the median wealth of white households was twenty times that of black households and eighteen times that of Hispanic households.[9] As theologian Ronald Sider, who has written on U.S. poverty for over thirty years, says, "We used to think of Europe as a class-based society in which aristocrats owned most of the wealth. Today, wealth distribution is more equal in Europe than in the 'land of the free.' The United States has the greatest income inequality of all developed nations."[10]

In the absence of safety nets developed during the 1960s' War on Poverty and later dismantled in the 1980s and 1990s, sights not seen in the United States since the Great Depression abound in our cities: shelters for the homeless, meals for street people, and food banks. Indeed, in my home city of Providence, Rhode Island, despite the growth of beds in homeless shelters, at the time of this cold January writing, there are 156 homeless people, sleeping outside, without beds or shelters.

3.1 Rhode Island Food Bank truck in front of church

Data from the Rhode Island Food Bank (Illus. 3.1) indicated the 2011 need, in this small state with a population of 1.06 million people.

- Each month more than 55,000 Rhode Islanders sought food through the Food Bank's network of emergency food programs.
- Food insecurity grew from affecting one out of ten households in 1998 to affecting one out of seven households in 2011.
- 41 percent of pantry recipients choose between paying for food and paying for utilities; additionally, 32 percent choose between food and medicine or medical care.
- One out of every three people served was a child under the age of eighteen.
- 77 percent of all households served by the Food Bank's network lived below the Federal Poverty Level, or less than $22,050 a year for a family of four.[11]

Inequality matters. Great income and wealth differentials lead to health, education, and social welfare disparities; see the example of Rhode Island (RI) below. Proportionately, three times as many Hispanic and black children in Rhode Island grow up in poverty as do white.

**Economic Well-Being Outcomes,
by Race and Ethnicity in Rhode Island, 2011**

	White	Hispanic	Black
children in poverty	12%	38%	30%
births to mothers with less than 12 years of education	14%	35%	22%
% of children with all resident parents in the workforce	71%	48%	65%
median family income	$77,093	$36,635	$41,469
homeownership	67%	30%	36%

There is appalling need and inequality in the United States. In the Two-Thirds World without subsidized housing, food stamp programs, or food banks, there is absolute chronic poverty, which means death from malaria, malnutrition, tuberculosis, and childbirth. Globally, 42 percent of the world's people (2.7 billion people) live on less than $2 a day; 24 percent live on less than $1 a day. The number of people who live in absolute poverty has increased over the last ten years. A third of all children in developing countries are chronically malnourished; that figure reaches 48 percent in South Central Asia and Eastern Africa.

While in Bangladesh in 1996, I visited with this family living a few miles outside the capital, Dhaka (Illus. 3.2). There was no electricity or indoor or outdoor plumbing. The women cooked over an open fire on the dirt floor (on the left in the photo) and washed their few clothes in the canal. Malnourished children gathered water from the village well; men worked in the fields seven days a week. A sister of the young mother worked in the Dhaka garment factories that made fashionable clothes for Americans.

Americans have believed that the United States is a very generous donor to the global poor such as this family. The reality is different. Foreign aid began after World War II with the Marshall Plan, which provided $13 billion for recovery to sixteen Western European countries from 1948 to 1951.[12] Over the following years, levels of foreign aid rose and fell depending upon world events, including fears of communism and concern for stable allies in the Middle East. Middle-income Israel, with a population of 7.5 million in 2010, has been the

3.2 Bangladesh family

single largest recipient of foreign aid, receiving an estimated $114 billion dollars from 1949 to 2008.[13] For 2010, the United Sates provided $2.8 billion to Israel for military funding alone, the largest such grant in U.S. history and part of a $30 billion commitment over ten years.[14] In contrast, since its independence in 1971, Bangladesh (among the poorest countries in the world, with a population over twenty times that of Israel) has received $5.5 billion, or one-twentieth as much as Israel. Our birthplace, race, class, and gender are critical determinants of whether we will live in poverty, comfort, or affluence.

Political Power: The Control of Organizations and Institutions

Prior to the terrorist attacks of September 11, 2001, U.S. foreign aid fell to its lowest level since 1948.[15] Since then, foreign aid has soared, principally to allies in the Middle East (including Jordan and Lebanon), new allies in the former Soviet states, nations critical to the Iraq and Afghan wars (Pakistan), and to African countries in the "arc of instability" (Sudan, Ethiopia, and Liberia).[16] Foreign aid in the American Empire has been "modernized" and redefined as one of three pillars of national foreign policy, together with diplomacy and defense.

American funding and use of foreign aid reflects political power, which is the power of individuals, institutions, and countries to control or to sway the policies, laws, and norms of societies, states, and countries. Political power is "soft power," meant to influence outcomes through persuasion, inducements, and legal formalities. Such power goes on every day, all around us, in the public square and in the back corridors of power as individuals, lobbies, religious bodies, political parties, corporations, and the U.S. government itself seek to mold society to their goals, values, and norms. Such power is exercised within the United States and across our borders. We feel the impact daily, without consciously identifying that the rules, laws, and norms by which we live were crafted by individuals or institutions to serve their goals, values, and norms. We may assume that such laws and norms are "just the way things are" or even the way things should be because the powers that be say they should be.

Sometimes societal goals, values, and norms promote the kingdom of God. Sometimes they do not. In Mark's Gospel, Jesus repeatedly confronts powers that oppressed, isolated, and devalued the poor, the vulnerable, the widow, and the orphan. He challenges the Great Tradition, with its traditions and powers that led to poverty and kept people in poverty, through healing on the Sabbath, disregarding purity laws, and overturning the tables of the money-changers in the temple. He promotes the Little Tradition, and the calls of Israelite prophets for justice and mercy, by telling parables that reverse the way things are, by performing healings that bring wholeness to the outcast, and by living out an inclusive love. Jesus is crucified, the Roman punishment for provincial rebels, for challenging political power that was contrary to the kingdom of God. His followers look for him back where he started with his disciples: in places of oppression, need, and despair.

In the 1960s, working with a national political will to reduce poverty, President Lyndon B. Johnson declared a War on Poverty. Over ten years, thanks to new programs, American poverty was reduced from 22 percent of the population to 12 percent. Over twenty years, beginning in the early 1980s, however, the government weakened or dismantled programs supporting the War on Poverty, and both the absolute numbers of the poor and the percentage of the poor grew.

By 2012, a study conducted by the National Academy of Science,

U.S. Health in International Perspective: Shorter Lives, Poorer Health, concluded that American health had declined relative to the health of other First World citizens, identified in the study as sixteen "peer" countries.[17] Infant mortality was higher in the United States than in the other sixteen countries; American children are more likely to die before their fifth birthday than children in any other of the peer countries. Life expectancy for men in the United States is the lowest of the seventeen countries, for women next to last. Within the United States, large health disparities exist. Researchers found that 17 percent of "U.S. counties has a male life expectancy that was more than 30 years behind that of the top 10 countries." Black infants are more than twice as likely as white infants to die before the age of one year.[18] The researchers comment:

> Disadvantages that exist in the United States relative to other countries are all the more remarkable given the size and relative wealth of the U.S. economy and the nation's enormous spending on health care. Health care expenditures in the United States have grown from . . . 9.2 percent of gross national product (GDP) in 1980 to . . . 17.9 percent of GDP in 2010. . . . No other country in the world spends as much on health care, and per capita spending on health care is also much higher in the United States than in any other country.[19]

At the same time, the United States has the highest poverty rate and the highest child poverty rate of the seventeen countries. The authors conclude that a variety of interrelated social and economic factors explain the huge American investment in health care and the relatively (to peer counties) poor health outcomes: high poverty and child poverty rates, high income inequality, "highest rates of incarceration among high income countries and the highest rate of households with children headed by a single parent."[20]

Political power, reflecting the power of class, race, and gender, is a determining factor of who is poor and who stays poor. Women have historically fared badly. In the United States, the poorest of the poor are single women with children in urban areas with poor high schools; few choices for teens; and little support for further education, training, or child care. As single moms, without child care and with few employment opportunities, they are triply vulnerable and disproportionately the victims of sexual and domestic violence.[21] In the Gospel of Mark, Jesus gives new life to such a vulnerable woman, who had previously sought help in vain (5:25-34). Power and liberation come for her as she defies the societal norms of her culture.

Place and borders, geographic and cultural, figure prominently in the Gospel of Mark. Jesus was a border crosser. So are Christians today. In a 2007 solidarity meeting I attended, Christians rallied behind undocumented immigrants in New Bedford, Massachusetts, thirty miles from Plymouth, where the seventeenth-century Pilgrims (my ancestors included) had arrived, uninvited, on the Native American shore. The Immigration and Customs Enforcement authorities had seized 361 undocumented Latino workers, mainly women, at a New Bedford factory that made clothing and leather goods for the American military (Illus. 3.3). Most of the women were sent to detention centers, many out of the state, leaving over one hundred children stranded when their seized mothers did not return home. A United

3.3 Solidarity meeting in New Bedford

Methodist pastor who was at one detention center when the detainees arrived reported that the women, many of them teenagers, departed from the bus with chains running from their wrists to their waists to their ankles.[22]

In a world of extreme imbalance between the rich and the poor, immigration policy is a critical factor in enabling or denying better lives for the poor, such as the women in New Bedford. As the United Nations Development Report for 2009 noted, "Our world is very unequal. For many people around the world moving away from their home town or village can be the best—sometimes the only—option open to improve their life chances. Migration can be hugely effective in improving the income, education and participation of individuals and families, and enhancing their children's future prospects."[23] The American government, however, works hard to prevent unauthorized entry into the country. Immigration is biased in favor of formally educated people with professional skills and those with significant funds to invest in the United States.[24]

Borders and barricades are hallmarks of empire; selectively porous, they define who's in and who's out, what passes and what is prohibited. In modern empire, investment, trade, commerce, and communication flow easily across borders. Factories are moved from Mexico to the Philippines to China for greater profit. Girls from Southeast Asia and the former Soviet states are enslaved, drugged, and trafficked for prostitution across the world. But poor people searching for a better life have a harder time successfully crossing those borders; thousands annually attempt to cross the American/Mexican border and tragically fail. In 2010 alone, border authorities found 252 bodies of Mexican and Central American migrants in the desert and mountains north of the border. Across the Atlantic, it is a similar story; North African migrants crowd overloaded boats for the risky ride across the Mediterranean and new life in Europe, often only to lose their lives or to end up in camps for the undocumented on both sides of the crossing. Women of Southeast Asia cross borders seeking employment in wealthy Arab states; finding abuse and misery, they end up trapped, with passports gone, borders closed, and freedom denied. Jesus speaks good news to those people, poor and rich, who are entrapped by the politics and borders of their culture; for those with "ears to hear," he speaks the liberating good news of the king-dom of God.

Military Power: Vast Military Might around the World

The word "military" brings different images to mind, depending on our backgrounds and social locations. I am the daughter of an army officer who fought across Europe in World War II; I lived on an army base as a child and still look fondly on men and women in uniform. I remember my father's story of his encountering, early in the war, bare-foot men arriving by train from Appalachia, reporting for duty in a New England winter and eager to serve their country. The military consists of men and women wanting to serve, wanting a chance to bet-ter themselves in life through the education and training the military offers, and fighting because they believe it is their best or only choice.

The military power of empire, on the other hand, is a different thing. It is the cumulative result of ideological, political, and economic decisions about global power, control of resources, values, and gods. Chalmers Johnson gives a good example of how such power works in his discussion of the 1979 American secret aid to the opponents of the pro-Soviet regime in Kabul, Afghanistan, which bordered the then-Soviet Union and which was a traditional sphere of Soviet influ-ence. Citing the memoir of former CIA Director Robert Gates and an interview with former United States national security advisor Zbig-niew Brzezinski, Johnson reveals that American intelligence services armed radical Islamic anti-Soviet guerillas for six months before the Soviets invaded the country, partly in response to the turmoil gen-erated by the U.S.-funded guerilla activities. The result was civil war in Afghanistan, troubles for the Soviet Union that contributed to its demise, and the further development of radical Islam and al-Qaeda. Two years after the Soviet invasion, Brzezinski was asked if he regret-ted the American intervention in Afghanistan. He replied, "Regret what? The secret operation was an excellent idea. It drew the Russians into the Afghan trap and you want me to regret it? On the day that the Soviets officially crossed the border, I wrote to President Carter, saying, in essence, 'We now have the opportunity of giving to the USSR its Vietnam War.'"[25]

That civil war led to the Afghan tragedy: as of 2010, it included "1.8 million Afghan casualties, 2.6 million refugees, and 10 million unexploded land mines."[26] In time, the support for radical Islam and the fundamentalist al-Qaeda would lead down a tragic path to the forces that struck the United States on September 11, 2011; the effects of that "blowback," or negative reactions carried out by the CIA and other covert operations, continue as we fight our own war in Afghanistan.

The United States, the most powerful nation in history, fights guerrillas in one of the least developed nations on earth today. We do so from a position that Barry R. Posen calls "command of the commons," denoting American command of the earth's public spaces of water, air, and sea; such command is based both on vast superiority in economic resources and on willingness to spend those resources on armaments.[27] Posen points out that in 2003 the United States produced 23 percent of the gross world product (GWP); the next two most economically powerful nations are China with 10 percent and Japan with 7. The amount of money the United States devoted to defense—3.5 percent of our gross national product—was nearly one percent of the world's GWP.[28] The result is a sophistication of warfare far beyond the imagination of the average American and closer to the realm of *Star Wars* movies. United States–based military technicians can go to war in the morning, operating remote-controlled death-causing drones in Afghanistan, and return home in the afternoon to play soccer with their kids in suburban America.

Command of the commons is the military foundation of American Empire. Posen writes that it has allowed the United States to exploit more fully other forms of power of its own and of its allies, as well as offering the opportunity to "weaken adversaries, by restricting their access to economic, military and political assistance."[29] The latest Department of Defense figures indicate that the United States owns or rents 4,742 military sites (bases) within the nation, 121 bases on U.S. territories, and 716 military bases overseas in thirty-eight countries, for a total of 5,579 worldwide.[30] As Johnson points out, however, "The official figures omit espionage bases, those located in war zones, Iraq and Afghanistan, and miscellaneous facilities in places considered too sensitive to discuss or which the Pentagon for its own reasons chooses to exclude—e.g., Israel, Kosovo, or Jordan."[31] Johnson and other analysts estimate that the United States actually has military bases in 130 countries. The United States is the world's largest military spender, accounting for 43 percent of total global expenditures (estimated to be $1.63 trillion in 2010), seven times as great as follow-up China; the United States also leads the world in arms sales to other countries.[32]

"The army is at war, but the country is not," said David M. Kennedy, Pulitzer Prize–winning historian. "We have managed to create and field an armed force that can engage in very, very lethal warfare without the society in whose name it fights breaking a sweat."[33] The result, he said, is "a moral hazard for the political leadership to resort to force in the knowledge that civil society will not be deeply disturbed."[34] But disturbed many of us are. One profoundly disturbing aspect of empire and the exercise of its military might today is that American warfare is waged in weak, poor countries that are "contested zones"[35] in the battle for empire and are left further impoverished by the battle. Afghanistan, before the American arming of anti-Soviet guerillas in the 1970s, was a beautiful country in which my husband and I traveled with our young children. Walking with our Afghan friends in the valleys outside Kabul, we were greeted by children running out of their houses and yelling on behalf of their gracious mothers, "Come, come, have tea with us" (Illus. 3.4).

It is a world gone forever. Should we have intervened by funding anti-Soviet guerillas in the first place? Having done so, couldn't we have found a Christian way to respond to the tragedy we created in al-Qaeda?

On September 11, 2001, I was in Nairobi, Kenya, expecting to depart for home the following day. For several days previous, the public health team I had been leading had been in the Great Rift Valley of Kenya, where humankind evolved some five to seven million years ago. The Rift Valley was the cradle of homo sapiens, our species; however, the team found no swaddling clothes. There, the percentage of the population infected with AIDS was estimated to be 33 to 35 percent, mainly young adults.[36] There were few medicines to halt the progression of the disease or drugs to reduce the suffering of the dying. Groups of small barefooted children, many with infants strapped to their backs, trudged the roads. Children ate dirt to fill their empty stomachs. The year before, 180,000 Kenyans died of AIDS out of a population of 29

3.4 Afghan children, 1977

million people, a mortality rate thirty times that of the United States at the height of AIDS mortality in 1994.

The team arrived back at the hotel knowing nothing of al-Qaeda's attacks on Americans on American soil. The Kenyan hotel staff greeted us with genuine sympathy. They understood suffering. They knew what it meant to be the victim of al-Qaeda, which had driven a truck bomb into the American Embassy in Nairobi three years previously; over two hundred were killed and four thousand injured, all but a few of them Kenyan. In the days that followed 9/11, unable to return home because of the international travel ban, I avidly read the Kenyan English newspapers. The editorials particularly caught my attention. They condemned al-Qaeda's attacks, mourned the dead, and expressed sympathy for the wounded and the grieving. Then they asked, "What will America learn from this terrible tragedy? Will it understand the Two-Thirds World better? How will it use its great power to bring justice?"

The American preemptive attack, invasion, destruction, and incomplete reconstruction of Iraq was one answer to their questions. It has been a lost decade, with mounting inequality and hardship in the

United States and trillions spent on war. As the years pass with fewer images in the press, it is important to be reminded of the cost of warfare, lest we followers of Jesus become part of the civil society that is not deeply disturbed by warfare. Remember Fallujah: an ancient city of 350,000 people attacked over eight days by a Marine-led force of 10,000 Americans in 2004. News in the United States was minimal; I was in Egypt at the time and read the following in the Egyptian English newspaper:

> News from Fallujah has been scarce and one-sided. Even the photos are censored. The access road to the city is still closed. The only people allowed in are those working with the Iraqi Red Crescent. . . . According to well-informed sources, 600 bodies are still lying under the rubble in Falluja. Others have been dismembered by dogs, thrown in the river, or completely decomposed. Most buildings and markets have been destroyed. The city has no electricity, drinking water, telephone service, or sewerage network.[37]

Thirty-six thousand of the 50,000 homes in the city were destroyed. Later, we learned that the American forces used "white phosphorous," similar to napalm, in the invasion. In 2010, according to the United Nations refugee agency, there remained 1.5 million internally displaced persons in Iraq, 60 percent of whose homes have either been damaged or destroyed or are now illegally occupied by others.[38]

Many of us are disturbed by the total costs of this war, not only to Iraq but to the United States and its allies in this tragic venture of empire. As Joseph Stiglitz, 2001 winner of the Nobel Prize in Economics, wrote, "America has already paid a steep price for invading Iraq. The most visible burden is on our fighting men and women. The economic burden is less readily apparent. Current expenditures, largely financed by borrowing, have been grossly underestimated. . . . Future costs, which will continue to escalate after we finally leave Iraq, have been deliberately glossed over."[39] Stiglitz estimates that "the total budgetary and economic costs of the USA will turn out to be around $3 trillion, with the cost to the rest of the world perhaps doubling that number again." Three trillion dollars is an enormous amount of money, leaving behind so much trauma, pain, and misery. Tragic are the opportunity costs of those monies—the opportunities we had and passed up—to spend that money for the human well-being God wills.

Jim Wallis writes, "Brutality is the predictable consequence of domination, the inevitable result of empire, and an enduring part of the cycle of violence . . . domination is oppressive and corrupting for both the dominated and the dominator."[40] In the winter of 2004, over two hundred Christian leaders spoke out against the spirituality of empire and the "theology of war." Entitled "Confessing Christ in a World of Violence" and circulated by *Sojourners Magazine,* that confession is timeless. See an abridged copy in the Appendix of this book.

In the Gospel of Mark, Jesus gives us an alternative to the wilderness of empire.

CHAPTER 4

MARK 1 _____

Mark 1:1-8

> ¹The beginning of the good news of Jesus Christ, the Son of God.
> ²As it is written in the prophet Isaiah, "See, I am sending my mes-
> senger ahead of you, who will prepare your way; ³the voice of
> one crying out in the wilderness: 'Prepare the way of the Lord,
> make his paths straight.'" ⁴John the baptizer appeared in the wil-
> derness, proclaiming a baptism of repentance for the forgiveness
> of sins. ⁵And people from the whole Judean countryside and all
> the people of Jerusalem were going out to him, and were baptized
> by him in the river Jordan, confessing their sins. ⁶Now John was
> clothed with camel's hair, with a leather belt around his waist, and
> he ate locusts and wild honey. ⁷He proclaimed, "The one who is
> more powerful than I is coming after me; I am not worthy to
> stoop down and untie the thong of his sandals. ⁸I have baptized
> you with water; but he will baptize you with the Holy Spirit."

In a world in which the Roman Empire proclaimed Caesar as the son
of God, Mark proclaims a different son. The real son of God, Jesus
Christ, brings the good news of God's judgment, faithfulness, and care
for the vulnerable, as the Hebrew prophets proclaimed.[1] Mark says
that he is quoting Isaiah, in verses that theologian Walter Brueggemann describes as the "first clear, intentional case of the term *gospel* in
the biblical text, gospel as news from the outside system that is sunk in
loss and grief"[2] (Isa. 40:1-11):

> ¹Comfort, O comfort my people, says your God. ²Speak tenderly
> to Jerusalem, and cry to her that she has served her term, that her
> penalty is paid, that she has received from the Lord's hand double
> for all her sins. ³A voice cries out: "In the wilderness prepare the
> way of the Lord, make straight in the desert a highway for our

God. [4]Every valley shall be lifted up, and every mountain and hill be made low; the uneven ground shall become level, and the rough places a plain. [5]Then the glory of the Lord shall be revealed, and all people shall see it together, for the mouth of the Lord has spoken." [6]A voice says, "Cry out!" And I said, "What shall I cry?" All people are grass, their constancy is like the flower of the field. [7] The grass withers, the flower fades, when the breath of the Lord blows upon it; surely the people are grass. [8]The grass withers, the flower fades; but the word of our God will stand forever. [9]Get you up to a high mountain, O Zion, herald of good tidings; lift up your voice with strength, O Jerusalem, herald of good tidings, lift it up, do not fear; say to the cities of Judah, "Here is your God!" [10]See, the Lord God comes with might, and his arm rules for him; his reward is with him, and his recompense before him. [11]He will feed his flock like a shepherd; he will gather the lambs in his arms, and carry them in his bosom, and gently lead the mother sheep.

In proclaiming the good news of Jesus, Mark challenges Roman propaganda by co-opting Roman terminology that used the Greek word translated here as "good news" (also translated as "gospel") to announce a Roman military victory. As Myers writes, "Mark is taking dead aim at Caesar and his legitimizing myths. From the very first line, Mark's literary strategy is revealed as subversive. Gospel is not an inappropriate title for this story, for Mark will indeed narrate a battle. But the 'good news' of Mark does not herald yet another victory by Rome's armies; it is a declaration of war upon the political culture of the empire."[3]

Wilderness is a critical place of discernment in Hebrew tradition, a "place in biblical rhetoric where there are no viable life support systems. 'Grace' is the occupying generosity of God that redefines the place."[4] John the Baptist's dress and work invoke such grace and the image of the prophet Elijah, "a hairy man with a belt around his waist" (2 Kgs. 1:8) who fled to the wilderness and experienced God (1 Kgs. 19:4-9). In the Exodus story, when the people cried out in hunger to Yahweh in the wilderness journey, God answered with quail and bread. Grace abounds. To Moses, God says,

I have heard the complaining of the Israelites; say to them, "At twilight you shall eat meat, and in the morning you shall have your fill of bread; then you shall know that I am the Lord your God." In the evening quails came up and covered the camp; and in the morning there was a layer of dew around the camp. When the layer of dew lifted, there on the surface of the wilderness was a fine flaky substance, as fine as frost on the ground. When the Israelites saw it, they said to one another, "What is it?" For they did not know what it was. Moses said to them, "It is the bread that the Lord has given you to eat." (Exod. 16:12-15)

In Mark, people experience grace and radical change after the long walk from Jerusalem to the Jordan, through a rough, rocky, and wild terrain. It would have been an arduous sacrificial journey for people to come to John for a "baptism of repentance for the forgiveness of sins." Literally in the Greek in which Mark wrote, John calls for an "immersion of mind change for sending off of sins."[5] Crowds of people—"the whole Judean countryside" and "all of Jerusalem"—journey to the Jordan for a change of mind and a new way of life. The word "repentance" comes from the Greek *metanoia,* which means more than repent; *metanoia* means transformation. Sometimes forgiveness is translated as remission, which comes from the Indo-European root *smeit,* meaning to throw, send off.[6]

Like Isaiah, Mark depicts John's heralding good news of a new world order. Invoking Isaiah 40, John announces that one more powerful than he is coming after him; the Lord who follows after him will baptize with the power of the Holy Spirit. Power and authority will be central themes in Mark, as they are in empire. However, whereas empires use power for individual, corporate, and imperial aggrandizement, Mark foreshadows here Jesus' use of power to defeat Satan and to enable the steadfast love, justice, and righteousness of God.

The journey is a key metaphor of Christian discipleship. Mark begins his Gospel with the proclamation that this Gospel is only the beginning of the good news of Jesus Christ. He ends it with the promise that Jesus is with us and going before us. The good news is that Jesus is on the journey with us, wherever that may take us.

Sometimes it is to unexpected places. In 2008, believing that the good news of Jesus Christ is for all people, regardless of race, class, gender, sexual orientation, national origin, or legal status, members and

4.1 Communion in front of Wyatt Detention Center

friends of the Open Table of Christ United Methodist Church demonstrated outside the Wyatt Detention Center, a private prison in Rhode
Island, shortly after the death of Mr. Jason Ng, who had been incarcer-
ated there (Illus. 4.1).

An undocumented Chinese immigrant, Mr. Ng died after months of
pain and misery that prison authorities ignored; he had both untreated
liver cancer and a fractured spine because of physical abuse when
he was finally brought to a hospital a few days before his death. The
church helped to generate publicity about the denial of medical care
and his death. Efforts by many, church and secular, led to the removal
of all undocumented immigrants from the prison, an investigation into
care there and in other prisons holding the undocumented, lawsuits
against those responsible, and discussion in Congress about treatment
of undocumented immigrants. Four years after his death, the Wyatt
Detention Center, the U.S. Immigration and Customs Enforcement,
and five other defendants agreed to a multimillion dollar settlement on

his family's wrongful-death lawsuit in a United States District Court. It was a measure of justice after so much indifference, denial, and cruelty.

Mark 1:9-13

⁹In those days Jesus came from Nazareth of Galilee and was baptized by John in the Jordan. ¹⁰And just as he was coming up out of the water, he saw the heavens torn apart and the Spirit descending like a dove on him. ¹¹And a voice came from heaven, "You are my Son, the Beloved; with you I am well pleased." ¹²And the Spirit immediately drove him out into the wilderness. ¹³He was in the wilderness forty days, tempted by Satan; and he was with the wild beasts; and the angels waited on him.

"From Nazareth of Galilee" tells us that Jesus was from the margins, the north, where in recent years there had been rebellions against Rome. A Jew from the margins of a country occupied by imperial Rome—and for him, Mark says, the heavens are torn open and God's Spirit descends! "You are my Son, whom I love; with you I am well pleased." In this baptism, Jesus hears God's voice and is empowered to go forth, despite the arrival of Satan.

Some of us may struggle with the idea of Satan as traditionally represented—a male being with horns, dressed in red, with a long tail curling up to meet a pitchfork. Such an image personifies and projects evil outward, onto other beings and other people, an ancient way of handling the evil or sin in ourselves and in others. Theologian Walter Wink, who has written powerfully on the principalities and powers of the world, offers different images of Satan, demons, and angels. Wink points out two biblical understandings of Satan. The first, dating from the Hebrew Testament in which Satan appears only three times, is that of Satan as a "servant of God" who forces humans to make difficult decisions; Satan is not demonic, but is "more a function ('the adversary') than a personality."⁷

In this first appearance of Satan in Mark, Satan appears in the role of adversary, forcing Jesus to face terribly tough questions and make life-and-death decisions. Jesus could be asking himself what God is asking of him, as God's beloved son. In the face of Roman terror and oppression, what will it mean to follow in the footsteps of Isaiah? Where and what is the realm of God in a world of Roman exploitation, elite collusion, and peasant poverty? Here, Satan can be understood as a servant of God; angels will also come to serve Jesus.

The second understanding of Satan as the personification of evil comes later in Judaic-Christian theology and in this gospel itself. As Wink writes, "It is only in the period between the Testaments and even more in the period of the New Testament and early church, that Satan gains recognition. Soon he will become the Enemy of God, the Father of Lies, the Black One, the Arch-Fiend, and assume the statue of a virtual rival to God." [8] Wink writes of the difficulty modern folk have in understanding such symbols of Satan.

> While the symbol may have fallen on hard times, the reality to which it gave expression has become all the more virulent. Satan did not begin life as an idea, but as an experience. The issue is not whether one "believes" in Satan, but whether or not one is able to identify in the actual events of life that dimension of experience the ancients called "Satan." Nor is the metaphysical question, Does Satan really exist? of any real urgency, unless the question is asked in the context of an actual encounter with Something or Someone that leads one to posit Satan's existence. [9]

Mark tells us that Jesus had an encounter with Satan, but during this time of tempting and spiritual turmoil, angels waited upon Jesus. Angels (and demons) are spiritual realities at the center of our individual and institutional lives; they are the "inner aspect of material or tangible manifestations of power." [10] An angel, which means "messenger" in Greek, is the spiritual power within individuals, institutions, and societies that works to facilitate the well-being of others. Demons, on the other hand, are "the psychic or spiritual power emanated by organizations or individuals or subaspects of individuals whose energies are bent on overpowering others." [11] Satan, angels, and demons are about power and how power is used!

Dr. Martin Luther King, Jr., said, "Power at its best is love implementing the demands of justice. Justice at its best is love correcting everything that stands against love." [12] Do the symbols of Satan, angels, and demons hold meaning as experiences of power used for love and justice or pain and injustice in your life? They do in mine. A private for-profit prison that ignores the cries of a pain-racked prisoner, such as Mr. Ng, is demon ridden.

Mark 1:14-20

> [14]Now after John was arrested, Jesus came to Galilee, proclaiming the good news of God, [15]and saying, "The time is fulfilled, and the kingdom of God has come near; repent, and believe in the good news." [16]As Jesus passed along the Sea of Galilee, he saw Simon and his brother Andrew casting a net into the sea—for they were fishermen. [17]And Jesus said to them, "Follow me and I will make you fish for people." [18]And immediately they left their nets and followed him. [19]As he went a little farther, he saw James son of Zebedee and his brother John, who were in their boat mending the nets. [20]Immediately he called them; and they left their father Zebedee in the boat with the hired men, and followed him.

The good news is that the kingdom, or realm, of God is near, today. God's realm—not Caesar's—is the ultimate power. Followers of Jesus would have clearly known the difference between the two. Caesar's kingdom, as experienced daily, was one of oppression, inequity, crucifixion, and enslavement. God's realm, as the Torah and prophets proclaimed, was one of justice, mercy, and peace. Isaiah described it as follows:

> No more shall there be in it an infant that lives but a few days, or an old person who does not live out a lifetime; for one who dies at a hundred years will be considered a youth, and one who falls short of a hundred will be considered accursed. They shall build houses and inhabit them; they shall plant vineyards and eat their fruit. They shall not build and another inhabit; they shall not plant and another eat; for like the days of a tree shall the days of my people be, and my chosen shall long enjoy the work of their hands. They shall not labor in vain, or bear children for calamity; for they shall be offspring blessed by the Lord and their descendants as well. Before they call I will answer, while they are yet speaking I will hear. The wolf and the lamb shall feed together,

the lion shall eat straw like the ox; but the serpent—its food shall be dust! They shall not hurt or destroy on all my holy mountain, says the Lord. (Isa. 65:20-25)

Jesus' calling of the four men with "Come, follow me" is the first of three invitations to discipleship in Mark. The Gospel does not identify Jesus "calling" any women: that does not mean Jesus did not call women. We know from the ending of this Gospel, and from other Gospels, that women were his most faithful followers. Mary Magdalene was from Magdala, a fishing port on the Sea of Galilee, where women as well as men were involved in "various aspects of the salting process. Their presence in Jesus' permanent retinue . . . might well be related to the fact that" they "were engaged in chores other than the purely domestic, making it easier for them to join a wandering charismatic prophet."[13]

As feminist theologian Elisabeth Schüssler Fiorenza points out, the Gospels are "interpretive remembrances," not "comprehensive accounts of the historical Jesus but expressions of communities and individuals who attempted to say what the significance of Jesus was for their own situations."[14] Remembrance in a patriarchal society, where social organization and power revolve around men, is focused on the thoughts and actions of men—unless women disrupt that status quo. In that patriarchal remembering, the Gospel presents only men as disciples— but women break through the text as committed followers who are faithful to Jesus' call from beginning to end. It will be a woman who recognizes Jesus as the Messiah about to die for his people and anoints him as king for burial. When all the male followers have fled, it will be women who follow him to the cross, who follow and watch where his crucified body is laid, and it will be women at the tomb to whom the angel speaks. Jesus calls us all, men and women from all walks of life, to come and follow him.

Mark 1:21-34

[21]They went to Capernaum; and when the sabbath came, he entered the synagogue and taught. [22]They were astounded at his teaching, for he taught them as one having authority, and not as

the scribes. [23]Just then there was in their synagogue a man with an unclean spirit, [24]and he cried out, "What have you to do with us, Jesus of Nazareth? Have you come to destroy us? I know who you are, the Holy One of God." [25]But Jesus rebuked him, saying, "Be silent, and come out of him!" [26]And the unclean spirit, convulsing him and crying with a loud voice, came out of him. [27]They were all amazed, and they kept on asking one another, "What is this? A new teaching—with authority! He commands even the unclean spirits, and they obey him." [28]At once his fame began to spread throughout the surrounding region of Galilee. [29]As soon as they left the synagogue, they entered the house of Simon and Andrew, with James and John. [30]Now Simon's mother-in-law was in bed with a fever, and they told him about her at once. [31]He came and took her by the hand and lifted her up. Then the fever left her, and she began to serve them. [32]That evening, at sundown, they brought to him all who were sick or possessed with demons. [33]And the whole city was gathered around the door. [34]And he cured many who were sick with various diseases, and cast out many demons; and he would not permit the demons to speak, because they knew him.

Jesus moves from the wilderness to the heart of the Jewish social order, the synagogue, on the Sabbath.[15] "Synagogue" was the Greek word for "gathering together" or "assembly." Although today the word "synagogue" means a designated physical place for Jewish worship, scholars believe that in Jesus' lifetime, the synagogue was any space in which Jews assembled as a congregation. "Unclean" people would have been unwelcome; deviance and illness were identified as sin and a lack of holiness. As David Rhodes writes, "Holiness was a core value of the Jews, as stated (by God) in the Law: 'You shall be holy, for I the Lord your God am holy' (Lev. 19.2)." Jewish society was organized to preserve God's holiness, and most Jews did their best to preserve the holiness of God's people.[16]

The man with the unclean spirit recognizes Jesus as the "Holy One of God." Considering the Jewish concerns for purity, is it surprising to find the unclean spirit (a demon) within the synagogue, at the heart of religious power? However, think what demons must have been present among the people as a result of oppression. What demons (traumas and terrors) must they have suffered as a result of watching their sons, husbands, or brothers be crucified? What traumas and terrors must they have had from losing family agricultural land and their livelihoods, because they could not keep up with the soaring tax burden? What brokenness must have been present among the community! When Jesus teaches in the community, the realm of God opens and the broken ones struggle for wholeness. Jesus teaches in a new way that gives hope "that the landscape of justice is not just a mirage or simply wishful thinking."[17] Wholeness is love and justice, together inseparable.

Mark writes that the people were astounded at Jesus' teaching, "for he taught them as one having authority, and not as the scribes." New Testament scholar William Herzog likens Jesus' teaching of oppressed illiterate peasants living under a brutal occupation to that of the consciousness-raising pedagogy of liberation theology today, and identifies Jesus as the "pedagogue of the oppressed."[18] In the teachings of Jesus, the "Holy One of God," people became subjects who were empowered to look critically at their lives and their reality and to act for freedom and wholeness. Demons are forced to emerge into the light, identified for what they are, and vanquished. The Indo-European root of demon is *da*, which means "to divide," while holy comes from the Indo-European root *kailo*, which means "whole" and "heal." The good news is healing and wholeness for those previously divided and broken.

Myers suggests that the "we" on whose behalf the demon speaks is the "voice of the scribal class whose 'space' Jesus is invading. The synagogue on the Sabbath is scribal turf, where scribes exercise the authority to teach the Torah. This 'spirit' personifies scribal power, which holds sway over the hearts and minds of the people. Only after breaking the influence of this spirit is Jesus free to begin his compassionate ministry to the masses."[19]

In the teachings of Jesus, demons are vanquished. I saw that process in Angola, oppressed and impoverished by five centuries of Portuguese demon-driven and demon-causing empire, including the deadly enslavement and deadly shipment of an estimated four million people, from Angola alone, in the transatlantic slave trade to the Americas. Many African Americans are descendants of those slaves, force-marched in chains from their homes and thrown into the packed holds of slave ships for the Middle Passage, where many died amidst the filth, disease, hunger, and thirst.

The good news is that the "Holy One of God" entered and still enters such demon-filled space and brings liberation and wholeness to the broken. In the nineteenth and twentieth centuries, American missionaries circumvented Portuguese prohibitions on foreign evangelizing and educational and health services for indigenous Angolans; they taught and healed from mission stations, disregarding Portuguese restrictions. Led by three men who were products of those mission schools, independence finally came in the 1970s, only to be followed by a twenty-seven year brutal civil war with international Cold War interventions by Cuba, Russia, China, the United States, and South Africa. Brother fought against brother, and large areas of the country were laid waste and planted with land mines.

In 2009 I visited Huambo, where some of the most sustained and heaviest fighting had occurred. The historic Congregational Dondi mission station, where nineteenth-century missionaries first provided medical services and high school education to indigenous Angolans, was a ruin, surrounded by land-mined high grasses. In the city itself, churches bombed and pockmarked with bullets stood witness to past service and to the demonic destruction of war, as seen here at the United Methodist church of Huambo (Illus. 4.2).

4.2 Huambo firebombed church

But demons and division did not have the last word. Peace and hope have finally come. Not far from the ruins of Dondi is new life. An interdenominational Protestant seminary, dormant during the civil war, is now producing pastors for the thriving, postconflict Angolan church. Land mines are being cleared. Health staff and patients walked through the war's rubble for health services at a public clinic I visited. The demons are being exorcised (Illus. 4.3).

Mark follows Jesus' authoritative teaching and exorcism of demons with a healing of Simon's mother-in-law, the first woman Jesus heals. Upon being healed, she begins to "serve them"; perhaps she got up from her sickbed, collected firewood, and made dinner for them. Or, understanding that the Greek word translated here as "serve" is also used to describe the actions of the angels in the desert with Jesus and the actions of the women who followed him to Jerusalem, it is likely Mark is describing discipleship. To "serve" in Mark's time would have meant diaconal service or perhaps service of the Eucharist. Myers notes

4.3 Walking through the rubble

that later in Mark (10:45) Jesus will say of himself, "The Human One came not to be served but to serve" and he writes that "both at the outset and at the conclusion of Mark's gospel, women, in a society which devalued them, are identified as the true disciples. . . . Mark is serving notice that patriarchal theology and the devaluation of women will be overturned."[20]

The patriarchal translation of Jesus' self-identification as the "Son of Man" is challenged by scholars as misleading. In English, the word "man" refers to human males. "But the Greek word man (*anthrōpos*) means 'human' as distinct from beast or god. It is a generic term that can apply to any member of the human species."[21] Myers translates the term as the "Human One," writing, "I think it speaks not only to the meaning of the original Hebrew metaphor, but captures well Mark's own presentation of Jesus as the true human being."[22] Do we sense God differently if Jesus identifies himself as the "Son of Man" or the "Human One"? As Sharon Thornton writes, Jesus could also be known as the "Suffering Righteous One because he acted without evil intent to serve the cause of justice through the power of love."[23]

Mark 1:35-45

> [35]In the morning, while it was still very dark, he got up and went out to a deserted place, and there he prayed. [36]And Simon and his companions hunted for him. [37]When they found him, they said to him, "Everyone is searching for you." [38]He answered, "Let us go on to the neighboring towns, so that I may proclaim the message there also; for that is what I came out to do." [39]And he went throughout Galilee, proclaiming the message in their synagogues and casting out demons. [40]A leper came to him begging him, and kneeling he said to him, "If you choose, you can make me clean." [41]Moved with pity, Jesus stretched out his hand and touched him, and said to him, "I do choose. Be made clean!" [42]Immediately the leprosy left him, and he was made clean. [43]After sternly warning him he sent him away at once, [44]saying to him, "See that you say nothing to anyone; but go, show yourself to the priest, and offer for your cleansing what Moses com-

manded, as a testimony to them." [45]But he went out and began to proclaim it freely, and to spread the word, so that Jesus could no longer go into a town openly, but stayed out in the country; and people came to him from every quarter.

Mark will relate three occasions in which Jesus departs to pray in solitude; on other occasions, Jesus speaks of prayer. Clearly, prayer was central to Jesus' life with God. Brueggemann, who likens prayer to an "open, frightening, healing world of speech with the Holy One,"[24] stresses that prayer is dialogue and interaction between partners.[25] The psalms, which Jesus likely prayed, are examples of that dialogue with God: sometimes joyful, sometimes despairing, sometimes angry, and yet always giving thanks to God in and through all things. Jesus' final words on the cross were prayer, the opening lines of Psalm 22.

After prayer, Jesus declared it was time to move on to neighboring villages and "proclaim the message." There he casts out demons and heals. "Jesus was a traditional healer who was interested in healing both illness and disease. Disease refers to what was physically wrong (e.g., leprosy), while illness refers to the social consequences of the disease (e.g., being cut off from family and friends.) This explains why Jesus' healings so often led to the restoration of those who have been healed."[26] The word "leprosy" covered any type of spreading skin disease, including Hansen's disease, incurable at that time, and curable diseases such as ringworm. Such skin diseases rendered the sufferer "unclean" under Jewish law, to be banished from the companionship of others with no contact with "healthy" people. Lepers were to move about in public, covering their upper lips, wearing torn clothes and with bared heads, and warning of their polluted presence with the cry, "unclean, unclean!"[27] Illness was understood to be a reflection of sin or impurity, thus warranting community exclusion.

Jesus rejects that understanding; in his ministry of solidarity with the oppressed and outcast, he represents the "inclusive graciousness and goodness of God."[28] Such solidarity was a threat to the civil order and the temple authorities who alone had the power to declare a person healed and clean. AIDS is our modern equivalent of leprosy, and in this global world, economics and geography place active AIDS

4.4 Ugandan girl at AIDS clinic

patients beyond the sights of most Americans. In the United States, African American teenage girls, predominately urban, have the highest rate of new HIV/AIDS infections; most cases will be diagnosed and treated. However, 67 percent of those living with AIDS live in Sub-Saharan Africa, where only 37 percent of AIDS cases are being treated.

This Ugandan girl was receiving treatment at a clinic I visited in 2009; at the time, donor funding for AIDS treatment at the clinic was ending. Without it, she has probably died (Illus. 4.4).

How hard it is to accept that children in Africa will die of AIDS for lack of drugs while in the United States we spend $40 billion each year on toys, clothing, and health care for pets! Can we pray for the "immersion of mind change" that would bring us closer to the "inclusive graciousness and goodness of God"?

In the story of the leper, the NRSV translation indicates Jesus sternly warned the leper as he departed. Myers indicates a strict translation of the phrase would be "snorting with indignation." "How are we to make sense of these strong emotions?" he asks. "They only make sense if the man *had already been to the priests,* who for some reason had rejected his petition. Deciding to make an issue out of it," Jesus sternly gives the leper orders not to publicize the miracle. Now the leper is to help confront the purity system that the priests run. A healed man, he is to make an offering as a testimony to (against) them. "Jesus' anger, then, is directed against the symbolic order of purity of which this man is a victim."[29]

CHAPTER 5

MARK 2

Mark 2:1-12

¹When he returned to Capernaum after some days, it was reported that he was at home. ²So many gathered around that there was no longer room for them, not even in front of the door; and he was speaking the word to them. ³Then some people came, bringing to him a paralyzed man, carried by four of them. ⁴And when they could not bring him to Jesus because of the crowd, they removed the roof above him; and after having dug through it, they let down the mat on which the paralytic lay. ⁵When Jesus saw their faith, he said to the paralytic, "Son, your sins are forgiven." ⁶Now some of the scribes were sitting there, questioning in their hearts, ⁷"Why does this fellow speak in this way? It is blasphemy! Who can forgive sins but God alone?" ⁸At once Jesus perceived in his spirit that they were discussing these questions among themselves; and he said to them, "Why do you raise such questions in your hearts? ⁹Which is easier, to say to the paralytic, 'Your sins are forgiven,' or to say, 'Stand up and take your mat and walk'? ¹⁰But so that you may know that the Son of Man has authority on earth to forgive sins" —he said to the paralytic—¹¹"I say to you, stand up, take your mat and go to your home." ¹²And he stood up, and immediately took the mat and went out before all of them; so that they were all amazed and glorified God, saying, "We have never seen anything like this!"

What an image: Jesus preaching to a jam-packed room, while overhead four men dig through the mud and thatch roof, tear open a hole like the hole in the heavens when Jesus was baptized, and lower their paralytic friend on his mat to Jesus. One can imagine dirt falling on the heads of all below; what a mess! Jesus sees not the mess, but faith, and heals the paralytic. The scribes see blasphemy and encroachment on their territory of sin management.

Sin in first-century Judaism was not necessarily an immoral act; a sinner could be someone who failed to keep either moral or ritual norms of purity. Sin was equated with impurity and debt, and it was difficult for the average poor person to fulfill the requirements of the ritual purity and debt codes that would both keep them from sinning, under Jewish law, and relieve them of their sins, once committed. Jewish law specified sacrifices to recompense for sins, under the direction of the priests, but they were expensive and a burden for the poor. As in the story of the leper, Jesus is giving the people a new route to wholeness.

Today paralytic diseases such as polio have been wiped out in most of the world. Other preventable diseases such as diarrhea, measles, and acute respiratory infections that are controlled in the First World kill 7.6 million children under the age of five each year in the Two-Thirds World, where over 170 million children are malnourished.[1] Many around the world are paralyzed or disabled by societal stereotypes and oppression because of their gender, sexual orientation, race, class, and legal status. In the Two-Thirds World, such stereotypes imprison persons even while infectious and contagious diseases sicken and kill.

The Universal Declaration of Human Rights, adopted by the United Nations in 1948, proclaimed that "everyone has the right to a standard of living adequate for the health and well-being of oneself and one's family, including food, clothing, housing, and medical care." What if the $800 billion that has been spent to date on the Iraq war had been spent instead on global health care? In the United States, the sinful discrepancy between the infant mortality rate of white and black infants might have been eliminated. With determined political will and billions of dollars, expanded access to the prevention, care, and treatment of HIV/AIDS would have been possible.

This photo (Illus. 5.1) shows the joy that can come with the arrival of such services, depicting Egyptians rejoicing at the opening of a government health clinic in one of the poorest parts of the country.

What stops us as followers of the Human One from working to ensure that all peoples are able to rejoice that the chains of illness and oppression have been broken?

5.1 Rejoicing in Egypt

Mark 2:13-17

[13]Jesus went out again beside the sea; the whole crowd gathered around him, and he taught them. [14]As he was walking along, he saw Levi son of Alphaeus sitting at the tax booth, and he said to him, "Follow me." And he got up and followed him. [15]And as he sat at dinner in Levi's house, many tax collectors and sinners were also sitting with Jesus and his disciples—for there were many who followed him. [16]When the scribes of the Pharisees saw that he was eating with sinners and tax collectors, they said to his disciples, "Why does he eat with tax collectors and sinners?" [17]When Jesus heard this, he said to them, "Those who are well have no need of a physician, but those who are sick; I have come to call not the righteous but sinners."

Table companionship served as both the heart of community and as a means of segregating those who could afford to abide by the rigorous purity and debt codes, the righteous, from those who could not, the unrighteous and sinners. Jesus walks into the division and declares that all are welcome at the table, most particularly those who are broken and outcast. Tax collectors, collaborators with the Romans, were despised; they served a different king, yet Levi walking away from his tax booth to follow Jesus is symbolic of the new understanding of the realm of God. What are the implications of this new table companionship for our church life today?

Mark 2:18-22

[18]Now John's disciples and the Pharisees were fasting; and people came and said to him, "Why do John's disciples and the disciples of the Pharisees fast, but your disciples do not fast?" [19]Jesus said to them, "The wedding guests cannot fast while the bridegroom is with them, can they? As long as they have the bridegroom with them, they cannot fast. [20]The days will come when the bridegroom is taken away from them, and then they will fast on that day. [21]"No one sews a piece of unshrunk cloth on an old cloak; otherwise, the patch pulls away from it, the new from the old, and a worse tear is made. [22]And no one puts new wine into old wineskins; otherwise, the wine will burst the skins, and the wine is lost, and so are the skins; but one puts new wine into fresh wineskins."

The Pharisees' previous two honor challenges of Jesus were on sin (Jesus' forgiveness of sin and table companionship with sinners); this challenge is over fasting and keeping Torah. Jesus responds by alluding to the Old Testament passage where God is likened to a bridegroom with his bride, Israel, whom God saves and vindicates, and in whom God rejoices (Isa. 62:1-12). Jesus likens himself to this bridegroom who continues God's saving and vindicating work. In the midst of the pain of first-century Palestine, Jesus affirms that the realm of God is life, here and now in the joyousness of a wedding. With the analogy of a wedding, a future-oriented event, Jesus at the same time gives hope for a future of joy.

New Testament scholar N. T. Wright suggests that Jesus saw himself enabling this realm, this wedding, by leading a reform movement of followers who mainly continued to live in their towns and villages and "who by their adoption of his praxis, his way of being Israel, would be distinctive within their local communities."[2] He points out that although there were many leaders and prophets in the first century, "In not one case do we hear of any group, after the death of its leader, claiming that he was in any sense alive again."[3] After Jesus' death, his followers will fast and then begin his ministry anew.

Mark has added the seemingly unrelated sayings about cloth and wine to comment on the difficulty of beginning anew. The people who questioned why Jesus' disciples didn't fast had a hard time understanding the new realm, or praxis, Jesus was living out in their midst. Forty years after Jesus' death, when Mark wrote this Gospel, Jesus' followers struggled for new life, with faith in Jesus as their Risen Lord, in the midst of the Jewish rebellion. Every generation of followers faces new wine and old wineskins, or the question of how to live into their faith in the particular circumstances of their lives and their community.

Mark 2:23-28

> [23]One sabbath he was going through the grainfields; and as they made their way his disciples began to pluck heads of grain. [24]The Pharisees said to him, "Look, why are they doing what is not lawful on the sabbath?" [25]And he said to them, "Have you never read what David did when he and his companions were hungry and in need of food? [26]He entered the house of God, when Abiathar was high priest, and ate the bread of the Presence, which it is not lawful for any but the priests to eat, and he gave some to his companions." [27]Then he said to them, "The sabbath was made for humankind, and not humankind for the sabbath; [28]so the Son of Man is lord even of the sabbath."

The Pharisees have recognized Jesus as a threat and have begun a series of honor/shame challenges, "highly visible contests held in public, often crowded spaces," to shame him. Such public challenges, which usually led to debates, were "zero-sum games" in which the winner prevailed at the expense of the loser; the crowd or onlookers decided the winner. Herzog writes that Jesus, who came from a humble background, gained honor among the crowds in Galilee because they "recognized him as a truthful interpreter of the Torah and a renewer of the covenantal community of Israel. Steeped in Galilean versions of the little tradition, or the Israelite traditions of Galilean villagers, he argued Torah with the representatives of the great tradition and challenged their interpretive hegemony as well as the prerogatives claimed by the temple. Jesus gained his public stature (he was called rabbi and prophet) one honor challenge at a time, one healing at a time, one exorcism at a time, and one parable at a time."[4]

At issue in this challenge was the temple's interpretation of the Torah to the hungry crowds of rural Galilee. While Roman and Judean taxation drove them deeper into debt, into loss of their land to those elites, and into work as day laborers, Israelite scriptures recognized the desperation of hungry people and acknowledged their right to food.

> When you reap the harvest of your land, you shall not reap to the very edges of your field, or gather the gleanings of your harvest; you shall leave them for the poor and for the alien. . . . If any of your kin fall into difficulty and become dependent on you, you shall support them; they shall live with you as though resident aliens. Do not take interest in advance or otherwise make a profit from them, but fear your God; let them live with you. You shall not lend them your money at interest taken in advance, or provide them food at a profit. (Lev. 23:22–25:37)

The crowds are listening and watching the debate over the interpretation of Torah and the Great and the Little Tradition. The theme of crowds begins in Chapter 1. "And the whole city was gathered around the door. . . . Everyone is searching for you . . . and people came to him from every quarter." Mark builds the theme in Chapter 2: "So many gathered around that there was no longer room for them, not even in front of the door; and he was speaking the word to them. Then some people came, bringing to him a paralyzed man, carried by four of them. And when they could not bring him to Jesus because of the crowd . . . the whole crowd gathered around him, and he taught them."

Through the crowd theme identified throughout the Gospel (thirty-eight times), Mark stresses the public nature of Jesus' ministry. Jesus was a public figure, teaching and healing the poor in a public renewal of the Little Tradition and the Hebrew scriptures. Myers quotes the work of Korean liberation theologian Ahn Byung-mu, who concludes that

Mark's Greek word for crowds (*ochlos*) was "analogous to the rabbinic expression 'am ha'aretz ('people of the land')," which came to mean by the time of Jesus, "the lower class, poor, uneducated and ignorant of the law." As Myers concludes, Mark's Jesus is one "who is continually surrounded by the poor, who attends their importune cries for healing and wholeness, and who acts not just to bind up their wounds but to attack the structures that perpetuate their oppression."[5]

What is the church saying to crowds today? Might we call the 40 percent of Americans who share in less than one-half of one percent (.03%) of the nation's wealth Jesus' crowd? Might we specifically call African Americans, who suffered historic sin in chattel slavery, reconstruction, and segregation, and who suffered disproportionately in the Great Recession, Jesus' crowd? The median household wealth of black and Hispanic households is just a fraction of white households. "The typical black household had just $5,677 in wealth (assets minus debts) in 2009; the typical Hispanic household had $6,325; and the typical white household had $113,149."[6]

How is your church responding to the crowds today?

CHAPTER 6

MARK 3 _____

Mark 3:1-6

> ¹Again he entered the synagogue, and a man was there who had a withered hand. ²They watched him to see whether he would cure him on the sabbath, so that they might accuse him. ³And he said to the man who had the withered hand, "Come forward." ⁴Then he said to them, "Is it lawful to do good or to do harm on the sabbath, to save life or to kill?" But they were silent. ⁵He looked around at them with anger; he was grieved at their hardness of heart and said to the man, "Stretch out your hand." He stretched it out, and his hand was restored. ⁶The Pharisees went out and immediately conspired with the Herodians against him, how to destroy him.

In the healing scenes in Mark, people must stand up, reach, stretch, and defy the social norms in order to be made whole. In the Museum of Chora in Turkey, I saw a fourteenth-century mosaic that beautifully captured the mutual reach and defiance of social norms. Jesus reached out to heal the man with the withered hand; the man had to lean forward and reach across a wall to Jesus. How direct their encounter was, both reaching to the other, while in the background, three others watched disapprovingly. Today, in like manner, women defy sexism, people of color push across racism, and homosexuals stand tall in the face of homophobia—inspired by this Son of Humanity who proclaims and brings life and wholeness to all. With whom and for whom do we need to stand up to be made whole? How much do we need to stretch to be made whole ourselves?

Jesus' question, "Is it lawful to do good or to do harm on the sabbath, to save life or to kill?" is a paraphrase of Moses' ultimatum to the Israelites before they crossed over the Jordan, into the "promised land."[1] "See, I have set before you today life and prosperity, death and adversity. If you obey the commandments of God . . . then you shall live. . . . But if your heart turns away and you do not hear. . . . You shall perish" (Deut. 30:15-18). The Pharisees would entrap Jesus with their challenge on the law, but Jesus responds that the greatest law is to do good.

In the second chapter of Mark, the Pharisees had accused Jesus of unlawful behavior (picking grain on the Sabbath). Now, they move to destroy him.

Mark 3:7-12

[7]Jesus departed with his disciples to the sea, and a great multitude from Galilee followed him; [8]hearing all that he was doing, they came to him in great numbers from Judea, Jerusalem, Idumea, beyond the Jordan, and the region around Tyre and Sidon. [9]He told his disciples to have a boat ready for him because of the crowd, so that they would not crush him; [10]for he had cured many, so that all who had diseases pressed upon him to touch him.[11]Whenever the unclean spirits saw him, they fell down before him and shouted, "You are the Son of God!" [12]But he sternly ordered them not to make him known.

Jesus refuses to be named and orders people and unclean spirits to be silent. Myers identifies Jesus' stance with "the tradition of the Exodus God who will not be named (see Exod. 3:2-15)." He "refuses to accept any of the honorific 'titles' given to him by opponents or friends. Instead, he names himself the 'Human One.'"[2] Jesus could not allow the unclean spirits to name him for "naming gives one power over the other person or thing."[3]

Moreover, as Myers points out, Jesus turns the tables on the demons and names them instead when the struggle between Jesus and evil (Satan, demons, and unclean spirits) culminates in the story of Jesus' defeat of Legion (Mark 5:1-13). After that point, the unclean spirits no longer challenge or speak to Jesus, and Jesus successfully defeats them (Mark 9:25), even at a distance (Mark 7:24-30). "At issue in Jesus' confrontations with unclean spirits, then, is who has the power to frame reality. According to Mark, exorcism is first and foremost the practice of unmasking the truth of a situation. As such, exorcism is fundamental to any movement of liberation, personal or political."[4]

Mark 3:13-19

[13]He went up the mountain and called to him those whom he wanted, and they came to him. [14]And he appointed twelve, whom he also named apostles, to be with him, and to be sent out to proclaim the message, [15]and to have authority to cast out demons. [16]So he appointed the twelve: Simon (to whom he gave the name Peter); [17]James son of Zebedee and John the brother of James (to whom he gave the name Boanerges, that is, Sons of Thunder); [18]and Andrew, and Philip, and Bartholomew, and Matthew, and Thomas, and James son of Alphaeus, and Thaddaeus, and Simon the Cananaean, [19]and Judas Iscariot, who betrayed him.

Crowds of people have come to Jesus from all over. Earlier, Mark identified five followers of Jesus. Now, there are twelve, symbolic of the twelve tribes of Israel. Mark has not identified any women as being among Jesus' closest companions in the renewal of Israel; however, as mentioned previously, that does not mean there were no women in the group. As Elisabeth Schüssler Fiorenza has pointed out, the absence of women in patriarchal texts does not mean the absence of women in the historical context.[5]

What a threat to Rome and to the temple this movement must have been. People come even from beyond the Jordan River to hear his message of the kingdom of God. Mark portrays the disciples as a rather weak bunch, perhaps as a narrative style to inspire the readers and listeners to Mark to be more faithful followers than the original disciples. However, think of the courage of those early disciples! Think of their audacity to hope that life could change, as they faced Roman oppression and the collusion of Judean elites. The naming of the twelve follows Mark's mention in verse 6 that the "the Pharisees went out and began to plot with the Herodians how they might kill Jesus." How much courage do we have in face of great odds?

Mark 3:20-35

Then he went home; [20]and the crowd came together again, so that they could not even eat. [21]When his family heard it, they went out to restrain him, for people were saying, "He has gone out of his mind." [22]And the scribes who came down from Jerusalem said, "He has Beelzebul, and by the ruler of the demons he casts out demons." [23]And he called them to him, and spoke to them in parables, "How can Satan cast out Satan? [24]If a kingdom is divided against itself, that kingdom cannot stand. [25]And if a house is divided against itself, that house will not be able to stand. [26]And if Satan has risen up against himself and is divided, he cannot stand, but his end has come. [27]But no one can enter a strong man's house and plunder his property without first tying up the strong man; then indeed the house can be plundered. [28]Truly I tell you, people will be forgiven for their sins and whatever blasphemies they utter; [29]but whoever blasphemes against the Holy Spirit can never have forgiveness, but is guilty of an eternal sin"— [30]for they had said, "He has an unclean spirit." [31]Then his mother and his brothers came; and standing outside, they sent to him and called him. [32]A crowd was sitting around him; and they said to him, "Your mother and your brothers and sisters are outside, asking for you." [33]And he replied, "Who are my mother and my brothers?" [34]And looking at those who sat around him, he said, "Here are my mother and my brothers! [35]Whoever does the will of God is my brother and sister and mother."

Jesus' family came to the house out of concern for him. It's not surprising that his family might think him crazy; standing out in acts of civil disobedience was to risk death. Although speaking or acting truth to power is faithful, it also leads to the cross. The scribes came to monitor that very civil disobedience. Accusing him of being demonic, the scribes seek to diminish and isolate Jesus. When power is threatened, it often responds by labeling its opposition the worst social group of the era.

In this parable of Satan and his house, Jesus declares nonviolent resistance to the oppressive powers of Rome and the Judean collaborating elites based in Jerusalem. While the scribes accuse Jesus of being Satan, Jesus counterattacks, saying he couldn't be Satan because he is challenging Satan. As Walter Wink writes, "'Satan' is the actual power that congeals around collective idolatry, injustice, or inhumanity, a power that increases or decreases according to the degree of collective refusal to choose higher values."[6] Satan here is the power in and around the Roman Empire, its legions, and its collaborators.

Further challenging the power of the scribes, Jesus says "Truly I tell you, people will be forgiven for their sins and whatever blasphemies they utter; but whoever blasphemes against the Holy Spirit can never have forgiveness, but is guilty of an eternal sin." Juan Luis Segundo writes, "What is not pardonable is using theology to turn real human liberation into something odious. The real sin against the Holy Spirit is refusing to recognize, with 'theological' joy, some concrete liberation that is taking place before one's very eyes."[7]

Think of the struggles for liberation taking place around our world and in our backyard—and the backlash against them by those who turn such liberation into something odious. One example is the immigration war that revolves around such concrete liberation. Calling immigrants who seek a better life criminals and terrorists is a modern example of labeling that seeks to isolate those seeking liberation.

The refusal to recognize liberation in our midst can be experienced in our homes. Think of attempts of women to get out of abusive relationships and the response to those attempts. Family and clergy may counsel patience or even accepting abuse as "bearing one's cross." Jesus' ministry is the opposite of such advice, however. Mark's stories portray Jesus and his followers reaching and stretching beyond social norms for liberation (3:1-6; 5:25-34; 7:24-30), by Jesus reinterpreting Torah to bring liberation (1:35-45; 3:1-6), and by Jesus' refusing to be defined by his hometown when he steps beyond their definition of his place (6:1-6).

The way of Jesus is justice with love, and Jesus identifies those who do God's will as being his mother, brother, and sister. Schüssler Fiorenza notes that although the narrative twice speaks of Jesus' mother and brothers, there is no mention of a father. She comments that Mark's Jesus holds up a community of equal discipleship, in contrast to the patriarchal family in which a father ruled and inequality reigned.

"Those who live the gracious goodness of God are Jesus' true family, which includes brothers, sisters and mothers, but significantly enough, no fathers. The exclusion of fathers from the 'true family' of Jesus cannot be explained by biographical reference or by reference to God as the true father of Jesus, since Mark 10:30 also omits fathers."[8] Schüssler Fiorenza and other feminist scholars theorize that these descriptions of Jesus' new family depict the earliest community of Jesus followers in which patriarchy, for a time, was not the basis of community.

CHAPTER 7

MARK 4 _____

Mark 4:1-20

¹Again he began to teach beside the sea. Such a very large crowd gathered around him that he got into a boat on the sea and sat there, while the whole crowd was beside the sea on the land. ²He began to teach them many things in parables, and in his teaching he said to them: ³"Listen! A sower went out to sow. ⁴And as he sowed, some seed fell on the path, and the birds came and ate it up. ⁵Other seed fell on rocky ground, where it did not have much soil, and it sprang up quickly, since it had no depth of soil. ⁶And when the sun rose, it was scorched; and since it had no root, it withered away. ⁷Other seed fell among thorns, and the thorns grew up and choked it, and it yielded no grain. ⁸Other seed fell into good soil and brought forth grain, growing up and increasing and yielding thirty and sixty and a hundredfold." ⁹And he said, "Let anyone with ears to hear listen!" ¹⁰When he was alone, those who were around him along with the twelve asked him about the parables. ¹¹And he said to them, "To you has been given the secret of the kingdom of God, but for those outside, everything comes in parables; ¹²in order that 'they may indeed look, but not perceive, and may indeed listen, but not understand; so that they may not turn again and be forgiven.'" ¹³And he said to them, "Do you not understand this parable? Then how will you understand all the parables? ¹⁴The sower sows the word. ¹⁵These are the ones on the path where the word is sown: when they hear, Satan immediately comes and takes away the word that is sown in them. ¹⁶And these are the ones sown on rocky ground: when they hear the word, they immediately receive it with joy. ¹⁷But they have no root, and endure only for a while; then, when trouble or persecution arises on account of the word, immediately they fall

away. [18]And others are those sown among the thorns: these are the ones who hear the word, [19]but the cares of the world, and the lure of wealth, and the desire for other things come in and choke the word, and it yields nothing. [20]And these are the ones sown on the good soil: they hear the word and accept it and bear fruit, thirty and sixty and a hundredfold."

Mark's chapter 4 begins and ends on the sea or lake of Galilee. In the Old Testament, the sea is a symbol of chaos; in the first verses of Genesis, God is depicted as subduing and ordering chaos, "which God orders by speech and enlivens by wind (spirit)." As Walter Brueggemann writes, "by utterance and by act," God "creates a life-world of order, vitality, and fruitfulness that makes life possible and that, in the end, is judged by God to be 'very good.'"[1] In like manner, Jesus by utterance (teaching, sayings, and debates) and by act (healing and exorcizing) makes abundant life possible for the oppressed and outcast with "ears to hear." A key way Jesus accomplished this was through parables.

Parables are riddles, meant to provoke discussion and thought. In the context of occupied Palestine, they were also a means for Jesus and villagers to talk in coded language and for Jesus to teach the villagers how to analyze their own reality. Herzog writes, "If parabling were part of Jesus' public activity that was followed with suspicion and eventually deemed actionable, then his parables must have dealt with dangerous issues, which always means political and economic issues, since the preservation of power and the extraction of tribute from the peasants dominated the concerns of the ruling elites of the ancient world."[2]

What issues in peasant life would a parable about predators (birds, sun, and thorns) and violent outcomes (devoured, scorched, and choked) bring to mind for oppressed peasants who were forced to give most of their harvest to local elites, the Romans and the temple? Herzog asks and answers that question in light of Jesus' execution by the Romans. The ravenous birds were the local elites who controlled their villages and who were the first to take whatever they could from the peasants. The sun represented the "scorched earth policies" of Rome, which demanded tribute on top of the taxes given to the local elites. The thorns were the additional predatory demands for tithes and taxes from the Judean elites and temple. In contrast to the peasants' reality, was God's word in the Torah that all land belonged to God. In the reign of God, all would share and no one would be poor. Their abundance would be "thirty and sixty and a hundredfold."[3]

The agrarian poverty and exploitation in the parable is similar to the situation under which many millions of people labor today. This Salvadoran coffee picker went to work as a small child on a plantation owned by one of El Salvador's landed aristocracy who had seized communal Indian lands one hundred years previously (Illus. 7.1). She worked in the fields ten to twelve hours a day for sixty years, earning barely enough to feed and clothe her family. Her home, when I visited her in 2002, was two small rooms, one of which she had turned over to the local health committee to serve as a baby clinic for the community. Her hands tell the story of a life of brutally hard labor; her act of sharing is a story of the reign of God.

7.1 Salvadoran coffee picker

In verses 10-12, the author of Mark interprets the parable for his community during the years of struggle and war against Rome. The question in that time and in every generation is, "What does it mean to be faithful?" How are we and our faith communities faithful? One exemplary response to the challenge of faithfulness is the Sudan project of Ginghamsburg United Methodist Church (UMC) of Ohio. Since initiating The Sudan Project in January 2005, Ginghamsburg UMC in partnership with the United Methodist Committee on Relief has raised and invested a remarkable $5.6 million in humanitarian relief in Darfur. The resulting agricultural project, child development program, and safe water initiative annually reach a quarter of a million Sudanese refugees and villagers in great human need. The agricultural yield in 2008 was eighteen bags of food for every seed planted.[4]

Mark 4:21-25

[21]He said to them, "Is a lamp brought in to be put under the bushel basket, or under the bed, and not on the lampstand? [22]For there is nothing hidden, except to be disclosed; nor is anything secret, except to come to light. [23]Let anyone with ears to hear listen!" [24]And he said to them, "Pay attention to what you hear; the measure you give will be the measure you get, and still more will be given you. [25]For to those who have, more will be given; and from those who have nothing, even what they have will be taken away."

One cannot have the reign of God alone. This message about disclosing follows directly after the parable in which Jesus says he has given the "secret" or mystery to his disciples. The analogy of a lamp makes it clear that "parables were meant to reveal, not conceal."[5] Parables were riddles to enable listeners to understand and critique the oppression in their lives. Today, public symbolic actions can act in a similar way to disclose what is hidden; the faith community plays a vital role in such actions. Freedom rides in the segregated South, marches on behalf of the undocumented in Arizona, communion services in front of prisons, walks against domestic violence, and other public symbolic actions serve to "Let anyone with ears listen."

In 2010, Beneficent United Church of Christ in Providence, Rhode

7.2 Walk a mile in her shoes

Island, hosted a walk, a public symbolic action, against domestic violence. For each of the previous two years in the tiny state of Rhode Island, ten women had been murdered by their current or ex-husbands or lovers. The previous year, the police responded to over 8,400 frantic calls for help because of domestic violence, 90 percent of it, male violence against their female partners. Young men and many others marched through the city streets in women's high heels in solidarity with women, revealing the abuse that is all too often concealed (Illus. 7.2).

Someday, having been brought into the light, domestic violence will become a global aberration. Does your church have a program to reduce domestic violence today?

Mark 4:26-35

> [26]He also said, "The kingdom of God is as if someone would scatter seed on the ground, [27]and would sleep and rise night and day, and the seed would sprout and grow, he does not know

how. [28]The earth produces of itself, first the stalk, then the head, then the full grain in the head. [29]But when the grain is ripe, at once he goes in with his sickle, because the harvest has come." [30]He also said, "With what can we compare the kingdom of God, or what parable will we use for it? [31]It is like a mustard seed, which, when sown upon the ground, is the smallest of all the seeds on earth; [32]yet when it is sown it grows up and becomes the greatest of all shrubs, and puts forth large branches, so that the birds of the air can make nests in its shade." [33]With many such parables he spoke the word to them, as they were able to hear it; [34]he did not speak to them except in parables, but he explained everything in private to his disciples. [35]

Humanity is in partnership with God, but it is God who decides the time and the size of the harvest. Sometimes we forget that in our efforts to make everything come out right by our own power. These parables, voiced in Mark by the "Suffering Righteous One," speak of the mystery of God. Myers comments that the image of shelter-offering branches is a metaphor for political sovereignty in the Hebrew Bible. In the book of Daniel, King Nebuchadnezzar dreams of "a tree at the center of the earth . . . its top reached to heaven . . . and the birds of the air nested in its branches, and from it all living beings were fed. The prophet promises that the hubris of empire will be judged and exhorts the king to 'atone for your sins with justice and for your iniquities with mercy to the oppressed.'" Jesus is an educator using language, images, and stories that peasants would understand from everyday life. In these stories, the world belongs to God. In such parables, Jesus "sows hope among them, insisting that the tall trees can be brought down and the smallest of seeds *will* bear Jubilary fruit."[6]

The story of the Jamkhed Comprehensive Rural Health Project (CRHP) in Jamkhed, India, is a modern story of a mustard seed and the reign of God. Founded by Dr. Raj Arole and his wife, Dr. Mabelle Arole, devout Christians brought up in mission schools founded by nineteenth-century American Congregational missionaries and trained in public health in the United States, the CRHP radically changed the practice and impact of global public health through the introduction of community-based primary health care among the rural poor. In 1970, with American mission support, they began the CRHP among the poor and marginalized populations of Maharashtra. Beginning in eight villages with a population of 10,000, "empowering people, families and communities, regardless of caste, race or religion, through integrated efforts in health and development," CRHP grew, like that mustard bush, to serve over three hundred villages with a combined population of 500,000.[7] Now, the CRHP training center receives 2,000 public health and development trainees per year from organizations in India and one hundred other countries.

In the early 1990s, with the support of the United Methodist Church, the Jamkhed model spread to Africa and Latin America, where I saw it in practice in the Belen Barrio of Iquitos, along the rivers of the Peruvian Amazon. A hundred years earlier, Iquitos had been an opulent center of the rubber boom (1880–1914), an international financial frenzy based on enslaved Indian labor on Amazonian rubber plantations. International corporations, the military, and the church each played a role in the horrific exploitation of the people; the rubber went into tires for the new automobile industry, and the wealth went to international markets and corporations.

Today, natural rubber comes from Southeast Asia, and Iquitos is an area of attraction for international tourists setting out on Amazonian adventures. In the Belen Barrio of Iquitos, descendants of the rubber

7.3 Iquitos, Peru

workers and other rural migrants live in one-room balsa wood shanties that float on the river and in simple houses on stilts. In the dry season the shanties stand twenty feet above the mud banks below. In the wet season the river rises twenty to thirty feet and flows through the barrio (Illus. 7.3).

Infant, child, and maternal mortality are among the highest in the hemisphere. Jamkhed-trained health workers, adapting the rural land-based Jamkhed model, move by canoe and on foot to deliver community-based primary health care. Because generations of Americans supported mission programs in India, Peruvians are being trained and are empowering families and communities along the Amazon. The reign of God is indeed like a mustard seed.

Mark 4:35-41

[35]On that day, when evening had come, he said to them, "Let us go across to the other side." [36]And leaving the crowd behind, they took him with them in the boat, just as he was. Other boats were with him. [37]A great windstorm arose, and the waves beat into the boat, so that the boat was already being swamped. [38]But he was in the stern, asleep on the cushion; and they woke him up and said to him, "Teacher, do you not care that we are perishing?" [39]He woke up and rebuked the wind, and said to the sea, "Peace! Be still!" Then the wind ceased, and there was a dead calm. [40]He said to them, "Why are you afraid? Have you still no faith?" [41]And they were filled with great awe and said to one another, "Who then is this, that even the wind and the sea obey him?"

The chaotic crossing of the sea may serve as a symbol for the struggle to move between the Jewish and Gentile world. The disciples struggled to cross borders two thousand years ago, and we struggle today. Myers writes, "Mark's harrowing sea stories suggest that the task of social reconciliation was not only difficult, but virtually inconceivable. No wonder, then, that in Mark's second boat episode Jesus must force the disciples to make the crossing (6:45)."[8]

CHAPTER 8

MARK 5

Mark 5:1-20

¹They came to the other side of the sea, to the country of the Gerasenes. ²And when he had stepped out of the boat, immediately a man out of the tombs with an unclean spirit met him. ³He lived among the tombs; and no one could restrain him any more, even with a chain; ⁴for he had often been restrained with shackles and chains, but the chains he wrenched apart, and the shackles he broke in pieces; and no one had the strength to subdue him. ⁵Night and day among the tombs and on the mountains he was always howling and bruising himself with stones. ⁶When he saw Jesus from a distance, he ran and bowed down before him; ⁷and he shouted at the top of his voice, "What have you to do with me, Jesus, Son of the Most High God? I adjure you by God, do not torment me." ⁸For he had said to him, "Come out of the man, you unclean spirit!" ⁹Then Jesus asked him, "What is your name?" He replied, "My name is Legion; for we are many." ¹⁰He begged him earnestly not to send them out of the country. ¹¹Now there on the hillside a great herd of swine was feeding; ¹²and the unclean spirits begged him, "Send us into the swine; let us enter them." ¹³So he gave them permission. And the unclean spirits came out and entered the swine; and the herd, numbering about two thousand, rushed down the steep bank into the sea, and were drowned in the sea. ¹⁴The swineherds ran off and told it in the city and in the country. Then people came to see what it was that had happened. ¹⁵They came to Jesus and saw the demoniac sitting there, clothed and in his right mind, the very man who had had the legion; and they were afraid. ¹⁶Those who had seen what had happened to the demoniac and to the swine reported it. ¹⁷Then they began to beg Jesus to leave their

neighborhood. [18]As he was getting into the boat, the man who had been possessed by demons begged him that he might be with him. [19]But Jesus refused, and said to him, "Go home to your friends, and tell them how much the Lord has done for you, and what mercy he has shown you." [20]And he went away and began to proclaim in the Decapolis how much Jesus had done for him; and everyone was amazed.

We are across the lake in Gentile territory, a region that Rome conquered and settled with army veterans in payment for their services. The Roman occupation, the image of a pig on Roman army shields, and the Jewish cultural code labeling tombs and swine as unclean are the setting for the story. In it, Mark attacks the Roman occupation in coded language. The tenth Roman legion, which carried the image of a boar (a wild pig) on its shields, had been stationed in the region since 6 B.C.E. Pigs do not travel in herds; rather "the term was often used to refer to a band of military recruits."[1] It is a scene "of profound impurity." The man is mentally ill; he is living in a cemetery, and pigs are feeding nearby. "The demoniac accurately depicts a condition of captivity to addiction or internalized oppression: he lives among the dead, crying out and engaging in self-destructive behavior." Myers understands this scene as offering a "symbolic portrait of how Roman imperialism was destroying the hearts and minds of a colonized people."[2]

"Only here in Mark does Jesus turn the tables on a demonic attempt to name him. . . . The answer Jesus receives to his demand for identification is stunning: 'My name is Legion, for we are many.' . . . In Mark's world this Latin term could only mean a division of Roman soldiers. Four such legions were based in Syria to control the eastern frontier, including Palestine. Yet this intimidating military force—in reality so powerful that 'no one could subdue' it," begged Jesus not to send them out of the country. Jesus gives the demons permission to leave. In Myers's words, "he dismisses them." The rush of a herd into the lake is an analogy to a military charge, like Pharaoh's army being swallowed up in the sea.[3]

After the healing, the people beg Jesus to leave; they are scared. Liberation can be scary and costly. Some people, through "colonization of the mind,"[4] can turn on themselves in self-hatred; others seek safety through conformity. In the impoverished villages of El Salvador, where in 2002 I took the picture of the elderly coffee picker who had toiled on plantations since a small child, Catholic liberation theologians in the 1970s and 1980s had animated the people to speak out for basic rights. There had been consequent brutal repression by the rightist government supported by the United States. Small apolitical Protestant churches began to grow. Salvadorans with whom I talked surmised that one reason for their growth was that peasants were seeking apolitical religious expression. Given the brutal repression and murder of activists, the liberation movement was too costly for some.[5]

Are there similarities between the fears of the oppressed and our own fears of what might happen to our lifestyles if oppressed people were free?[6] Are we afraid of what might happen to our lifestyles if *we* were truly set free? As Myers notes, "The power to exorcise demons in our society is grounded partly in having the courage and faith to face the demons that possess us personally. Having done so, we will always know their power, the agony they cause, and the essential role of community in exorcising them."[7]

Mark 5:21-34

[21]When Jesus had crossed again in the boat to the other side, a great crowd gathered around him; and he was by the sea. [22]Then one of the leaders of the synagogue named Jairus came and, when he saw him, fell at his feet [23]and begged him repeatedly, "My little daughter is at the point of death. Come and lay your hands on her, so that she may be made well, and live." [24]So he went with him. And a large crowd followed him and pressed in on him. [25]Now there was a woman who had been suffering from hemorrhages for twelve years. [26]She had endured much under many physicians, and had spent all that she had; and she was no better, but rather grew worse. [27]She had heard about Jesus, and came up behind him in the crowd and touched his cloak, [28]for she said, "If I but touch his clothes, I will be made well." [29]Immediately her hemorrhage stopped; and she felt in her body that she was healed of her disease. [30]Immediately aware that power had gone forth from him, Jesus turned about in the

crowd and said, "Who touched my clothes?" [31]And his disciples said to him, "You see the crowd pressing in on you; how can you say, 'Who touched me?'" [32]He looked all around to see who had done it. [33]But the woman, knowing what had happened to her, came in fear and trembling, fell down before him, and told him the whole truth. [34]He said to her, "Daughter, your faith has made you well; go in peace, and be healed of your disease."

In this "Markan sandwich" we have two stories, or one story interrupted by a second, related story: of a synagogue leader seeking help for his dying daughter, whom we will later learn is twelve years old, and of a lone woman who had been bleeding and seeking help for herself for twelve years. The number twelve unites the stories, as do the themes of health and wholeness. The man and his daughter are prominent people with proper behavior; the woman is an outcast with outrageous behavior.

Mark's depiction of a lone woman seeking out and touching Jesus would have been shocking on both the Jewish and Gentile sides of the lake. In patriarchal Mediterranean society, proper women were never alone in public. Public space was male space; the home and household were female space. Karen Jo Torjesen writes, "A woman's honor consisted in her reputation for chastity, understood as a sense of shame. Shame, the defining quality of womanhood, was manifested in passivity, subordination, and seclusion within the household."[8]

Since Jesus has crossed to Galilee, presumably this was a Jewish woman whose bleeding would have made her ritually impure under Jewish law. She would have been an outcast, contaminating anyone she touched. In touching Jesus, she is violating both the social rules of modesty and the religious laws of purity. Mary Ann Tolbert writes that with stories of women ignoring the social rules of modesty, Mark may have been challenging some of the restrictive cultural rules defining proper female behavior or possibly indicating the outcast status of some of the women attracted to Christianity. Jesus says "Daughter" and thus gives kinship to this woman, alone in the "male world of honor and shame."[9] What a beautiful act of grace.

This nameless woman is the only woman in the Gospels to seek help for herself. All the other women seek help for others, or have help

8.1 Bolivian woman in crowd

sought for them. She does not directly address Jesus, but reaches out to him, hoping to be healed but not to be noticed.

In the world of first-century Palestine, reproductive health complications and illnesses would have been the leading cause of death for women. Today, we don't talk about reproductive illnesses, although over fifteen million women suffer debilitating infections and injuries during pregnancy and childbirth. The woman, however, tells Jesus the "whole truth," the only instance in the Gospels where the Gospel writers give to one of the crowd the agency of speaking the "truth." Moreover, this woman, out of her suffering body, speaks "the whole truth!" She is trembling with fear as she tells him. What whole truth of pain and suffering would desperate women relate today if they had a chance and were not afraid of the repercussions?

With the symbolism of twelve, one might understand Mark 5:25-34 as a metaphor of salvation for the twelve tribes of Israel. I understand it as the salvation, or being made "whole," of one woman, and by implication, hope for all women who suffer because of their gender and sexuality, as they did in Bolivia, where I took this photo in a crowd thirty years ago (Illus. 8.1).

Most women delivered their babies at home, assisted only by traditional midwives. Family planning was illegal and unsafe, and illegal abortion was the leading cause of death for women. Other women lived with chronic infections and disability, similar to the woman in Mark's Gospel, from pregnancy and childbirth-related causes. Wealthy Bolivian women flew to Miami, Florida, for health care; but for poor women like these on the Altiplano, modern health services were no more accessible than they were for the desperate woman who touched Jesus. The "whole truth" is that services for *all* women, poor and rich, are an issue of justice.

Mark 5:35-43

[35]While he was still speaking, some people came from the leader's house to say, "Your daughter is dead. Why trouble the teacher any further?" [36]But overhearing what they said, Jesus said to the leader of the synagogue, "Do not fear, only believe." [37]He allowed no one to follow him except Peter, James, and John, the brother of James. [38]When they came to the house of the leader of the synagogue, he saw a commotion, people weeping and wailing loudly. [39]When he had entered, he said to them, "Why do you make a commotion and weep? The child is not dead but sleeping." [40]And they laughed at him. Then he put them all outside, and took the child's father and mother and those who were with him, and went in where the child was. [41]He took her by the hand and said to her, "Talitha cum," which means, "Little girl, get up!" [42]And immediately the girl got up and began to walk about (she was twelve years of age). At this they were overcome with amazement. [43]He strictly ordered them that no one should know this, and told them to give her something to eat.

What a commandment! "Do not fear, only believe." It is the prelude to the only resuscitation in Mark. The laughter of the crowd foreshadows the mocking laughter at Jesus' own death while the pronouncement that the child is not dead but sleeping is an imitation of Jesus' ultimate victory over death.[10]

CHAPTER 9

MARK 6 _____

Mark 6:1-6

¹He left that place and came to his hometown, and his disciples
followed him. ²On the sabbath he began to teach in the synagogue, and many who heard him were astounded. They said,
"Where did this man get all this? What is this wisdom that has
been given to him? What deeds of power are being done by his
hands! ³Is not this the carpenter, the son of Mary and brother of
James and Joses and Judas and Simon, and are not his sisters here
with us?" And they took offense at him. ⁴Then Jesus said to them,
"Prophets are not without honor, except in their hometown, and
among their own kin, and in their own house." ⁵And he could
do no deed of power there, except that he laid his hands on a
few sick people and cured them. ⁶And he was amazed at their
unbelief. Then he went about among the villages teaching.

Jesus' hometown was an oppressive place for him. The people said
with scorn, "Who does *he* think he is!" He doesn't know his place!
There is no mention of a father and his sisters have no names. Halvor
Moxnes, a Norwegian theologian, writes of the power of "place" in
our lives and Jesus' radical call that liberates people from oppressive
places in their lives. Place "does not just imply geographical location;
we may also, for instance, speak of social, ideological, or mental places
in terms of gender, ideology or power."[1] Moxnes, who is gay, knows
from whence he writes about the struggle for wholeness in the context
of society's attempt to shame those who have stepped out of society's
boundaries. He writes of Jesus:

> Jesus refused to be shamed into his (old) place within the village,
> to be bound by the honor-shame paradigm of the community. . . .
> Jesus, by presenting himself as a prophet, had rejected the order

and structure of the place. He was not acceptable within this place. He had placed himself outside this social location. His only option to come back into it was for him to accept his "place" in this social location as determined by genealogy, kinship, authority, subordination and the rest. But Jesus breaks out of the mold and will not be limited by the place defined by his lineage and household.[2]

What a powerful call to liberation for all oppressed because of their gender, sexual orientation, class, race, ethnicity, or background. As Mark relates in the next story, if one place is oppressive and unwelcoming to you as God calls you to be and to minister, move on!

Mark 6:7-13

[7]He called the twelve and began to send them out two by two, and gave them authority over the unclean spirits. [8]He ordered them to take nothing for their journey except a staff; no bread, no bag, no money in their belts; [9]but to wear sandals and not to put on two tunics. [10]He said to them, "Wherever you enter a house, stay there until you leave the place. [11]If any place will not welcome you and they refuse to hear you, as you leave, shake off the dust that is on your feet as a testimony against them." [12]So they went out and proclaimed that all should repent. [13]They cast out many demons, and anointed with oil many who were sick and cured them.

This is the mission charge for the disciples in the context of the hunger, illness, and suffering of the Jewish people under Roman occupation. Myers understands these instructions as Jesus' emphasis on the "utter dependence of the disciples for hospitality . . . they are allowed the means of travel (staff, sandals) but not sustenance (bread, money bag and money, extra clothes). In other words, they, like Jesus who has just been renounced in his own 'home,' are to take on the status of a sojourner in the land."[3] The text has lessons for us today, two thousand years later; our context is still one of hunger, illness, exclusion, and violence for millions in the United States and billions around the globe. The need for hospitality to the poor, the alien, the widow, and the orphan is as great as it was two thousand years ago. As Christians, we are people on a mission, called forth to serve in community, trusting in God, choosing to respond to Jesus' call in ways that meet our own deep needs and joys.

Mark 6:14-29

[14]King Herod heard of it, for Jesus' name had become known. Some were saying, "John the baptizer has been raised from the dead; and for this reason these powers are at work in him." [15]But others said, "It is Elijah." And others said, "It is a prophet, like one of the prophets of old." [16]But when Herod heard of it, he said, "John, whom I beheaded, has been raised." [17]For Herod himself had sent men who arrested John, bound him, and put him in prison on account of Herodias, his brother Philip's wife, because Herod had married her. [18]For John had been telling Herod, "It is not lawful for you to have your brother's wife." [19]And Herodias had a grudge against him, and wanted to kill him. But she could not, [20]for Herod feared John, knowing that he was a righteous and holy man, and he protected him. When he heard him, he was greatly perplexed; and yet he liked to listen to him. [21]But an opportunity came when Herod on his birthday gave a banquet for his courtiers and officers and for the leaders of Galilee. [22]When his daughter Herodias came in and danced, she pleased Herod and his guests; and the king said to the girl, "Ask me for whatever you wish, and I will give it." [23]And he solemnly swore to her, "Whatever you ask me, I will give you, even half of my kingdom." [24]She went out and said to her mother, "What should I ask for?" She replied, "The head of John the baptizer." [25]Immediately she rushed back to the king and requested, "I want you to give me at once the head of John the Baptist on a platter." [26]The king was deeply grieved; yet out of regard for his oaths and for the guests, he did not want to refuse her. [27]Immediately the king sent a soldier of the guard with orders to bring John's head. He went and beheaded him in the prison, [28]brought his head on a platter, and gave it to the girl. Then the girl gave it to her mother. [29]When his disciples heard about it, they came and took his body, and laid it in a tomb.

Mark interrupts the story of the disciples to relate the gruesome story of the death of John the Baptist. The placement of the story here, following the sending of the disciples into mission, stresses the difficulties Jesus' followers face in a world of rampant evil.[4] It forewarns of Jesus' own death. Mark's account of the death is, according to Myers, a "parody on the shameless methods of decision-making among the elite, a world in which human life is bartered to save royal face. . . . A more sarcastic social caricature could not have been spun by the bitterest Galilean peasant. . . . Above all, the story paves the way for Mark's supreme political parody, the trail and execution of the Human One by the collaborative Jewish and Roman powers."[5]

According to the first-century Jewish historian Josephus, Herod killed John for strictly political reasons: he feared his popularity with the crowds, and considered him to be one more insurrectionist. John gave the impoverished crowds, through repentance and baptism along the Jordan, a free alternative to the expensive temple rites in Jerusalem. Herod may have feared John would use that power as other prophetic Jewish leaders in that rebellious occupied land did. Clearly, however, the story of John, sandwiched here between the sending of the disciples and their subsequent recounting of their mission work, highlights the difficulties the disciples will face, then and today.

Mark 6:30-44

[30]The apostles gathered around Jesus, and told him all that they had done and taught. [31]He said to them, "Come away to a deserted place all by yourselves and rest a while." For many were coming and going, and they had no leisure even to eat. [32]And they went away in the boat to a deserted place by themselves. [33]Now many saw them going and recognized them, and they hurried there on foot from all the towns and arrived ahead of them. [34]As he went ashore, he saw a great crowd; and he had compassion for them, because they were like sheep without a shepherd; and he began to teach them many things. [35]When it grew late, his disciples came to him and said, "This is a deserted place, and the hour is now very late; [36]send them away so that they may go into the surrounding country and villages and buy something for themselves

to eat." [37]But he answered them, "You give them something to eat." They said to him, "Are we to go and buy two hundred denarii worth of bread, and give it to them to eat?" [38]And he said to them, "How many loaves have you? Go and see." When they had found out, they said, "Five, and two fish." [39]Then he ordered them to get all the people to sit down in groups on the green grass. [40]So they sat down in groups of hundreds and of fifties. [41]Taking the five loaves and the two fish, he looked up to heaven, and blessed and broke the loaves, and gave them to his disciples to set before the people; and he divided the two fish among them all. [42]And all ate and were filled; [43]and they took up twelve baskets full of broken pieces and of the fish. [44]Those who had eaten the loaves numbered five thousand men.

The scriptures relate God's abundance and faithfulness to poor hungry people who fear there will be no food for them. In the Exodus story of the Hebrews' desperate flight from slavery in Egypt, God provides manna in the desert, enough for each person and enough for each day (Exod. 16). But God allows no hoarding. A similar story is told of the prophet Elisha who, during a famine, feeds a multitude with twenty loaves of barley bread and had some left over (2 Kgs. 4:42-44).

What are Jesus and the prophets saying about the economics of food? That there is enough for all! That is true today. Despite deaths by the hundreds of thousands in the Two-Thirds World and food lines in the United States, there is no scarcity of food production in the world. Modern famine is not due to scarcity of food; the nineteenth-century Irish famine and the twentieth-century Bengal famine clearly demonstrated the geopolitical causes of famine. Today, Somalis, caught up in the barbaric civil war, starve or die trying to make it to the refugee camps over the Kenyan border. In the United States, while the rich have grown richer, the numbers of poor people at food pantries increases monthly.

The image of "sheep without a shepherd," through which Mark describes Jesus' compassion, was used by the prophet Ezekiel to indict rulers who only take care of themselves and who neglect or abuse their flock (Ezek. 34:1-10). Mark used it to contrast the leadership of Herod and the leadership of Jesus. Herod was abusive; Jesus was compassionate.

Jesus' compassionate feeding of more than five thousand people occurs in a setting described three times by Mark as "deserted." It was "very late" and must have been getting dark. Jesus and the disciples are exhausted, having had no leisure even to eat. In this deserted, dark, and wearisome spot, Jesus calls people to come together in groups. Together in groups, Mark's imagery changes, and they sit upon green grass. In groups they are fed and filled—community can bring blessings and bread into dark loneliness.

Community can bring blessings and bread into the darkness. It does in my home city. All year, three mornings a week before the sun rises, an appropriately named "Bread and Blessings" program serves coffee, muffins, and take-away bagged lunches to about three hundred homeless people in a church parking lot near Rhode Island's largest shelter for the homeless. Organized and managed by Franciscan Father Brice Leavins in collaboration with Beneficent United Church of Christ that provides the space, Catholic and Protestant volunteers come together with urban homeless men and women across the street, ironically, from a twentieth-century statue celebrating urban renewal. When I was there one icy winter dawn, a group of men clustered around a van and a man handing out coats and hats. One homeless man called out, "Don't push; there is enough for all."

This area of the city has both the highest percentage of the population living below the poverty line and the highest per-capita income in the city. High-rise, million-dollar condominiums look down upon the homeless in the park several blocks away. Although there are no longer camps of the homeless underneath the city's overpasses as there were a few years ago, a winter shelter assessment in December 2012 revealed 728 people in shelter beds, 112 on mats in seasonal shelters, and 156 living outside, most living within a few miles of my church and home.[6] What's happening in your community? How do we understand that 30 percent of Americans have no assets at all while 10 percent of Americans hold 70 percent of American wealth?

Mark 6:45-56

[45]Immediately he made his disciples get into the boat and go on ahead to the other side, to Bethsaida, while he dismissed the

crowd. ⁴⁶After saying farewell to them, he went up on the mountain to pray. ⁴⁷When evening came, the boat was out on the sea, and he was alone on the land. ⁴⁸When he saw that they were straining at the oars against an adverse wind, he came towards them early in the morning, walking on the sea. He intended to pass them by. ⁴⁹But when they saw him walking on the sea, they thought it was a ghost and cried out; ⁵⁰for they all saw him and were terrified. But immediately he spoke to them and said, "Take heart, it is I; do not be afraid." ⁵¹Then he got into the boat with them and the wind ceased. And they were utterly astounded,⁵²for they did not understand about the loaves, but their hearts were hardened. ⁵³When they had crossed over, they came to land at Gennesaret and moored the boat. ⁵⁴When they got out of the boat, people at once recognized him, ⁵⁵and rushed about that whole region and began to bring the sick on mats to wherever they heard he was. ⁵⁶And wherever he went, into villages or cities or farms, they laid the sick in the marketplaces, and begged him that they might touch even the fringe of his cloak; and all who touched it were healed.

This text abounds with Hebrew Testament metaphors. The disciples had to be made to get into the boat; the Greek implies they were unwilling to cross to the other side. Mark goes on to say, "Their hearts were hardened," a term meaning a resistance to change and God's revelation. In the Exodus story, Pharaoh's heart was hardened, and he yielded only after great hardship afflicted his people (Exod. 5:1–12:36). The Israelites finally escaped when God controlled and parted the sea for them (Exod. 14:21-31). In Jesus' first sea crossing while the waves crashed about, Jesus was asleep in the boat with the disciples, who were terrified (Mark 4:35-41). In this second sea crossing, undertaken at Jesus' command, they have still not learned to trust in him. In the midst of the chaos, Jesus speaks in the Old Testament language of revelation, saying "I am" to indicate God's saving presence.[7]

In today's empire, Christians, Jews, and Muslims seek God's saving presence in the chaos, suffering, and hardened hearts of the occupation of modern Palestine by the United States' key ally in the Middle East, Israel. Decades have passed since Israel seized East Jerusalem, Gaza, and the West Bank in 1967, and the occupation continues after both nonviolent and violent protest by the Palestinians to end the occupation. Over four million Palestinians live under permanent Israeli occupation, struggling with illegal Israeli settlements on Palestinian land, military watchtowers, Israeli water restrictions on the use of Palestinian water, and military checkpoints and road blocks. Densely populated Gaza, with 1.5 million people in an area less than 150 square miles, has been called "an open-air prison."

This military bulldozer for demolishing buildings sat outside the checkpoint to Bethlehem when I visited in 2002 (Illus. 9.1). In Bethlehem itself, scores of homes were rubble, and public services, such as sewage and electricity, were in shambles as a result of Israeli retaliation for a Palestinian uprising against the occupation. Less than a year after I took this photo, a similar vehicle crushed young American Rachel Corrie to death when she was peacefully protesting the demolition of a home in Gaza. Throughout the Two-Thirds World, the occupation and American defense of, and support for, Israel despite the occupation are key symbols of the American Empire.

Borders and barricades between the affluent global core and the poor periphery, such as Israel and Palestine, are conflict points in

9.1 Bulldozer outside Bethlehem

ten areas of the world. Geographer Harm de Blij, in his splendid *The Power of Place: Geography, Destiny, and Globalization's Rough Landscape,* maps those ten areas "where governments try to stem the tide of undocumented migrants moving from periphery to core," graphically illustrating "the power of place" in determining human well-being.[8] Borders are more complex than simply walls along a geographic border. The core prohibits undocumented persons from passing, but individuals, nations, and companies in the global core cross with ideological, economic, political, and military power. In occupied Palestine, Israeli settlers travel through the territory on roads reserved exclusively for their use, while Palestinians move from Israeli checkpoint to checkpoint, each garrisoned with Israeli soldiers. Through the military-industrial complex that Dwight D. Eisenhower warned about fifty years ago, American capitalism flows across these borders, and American companies profit from the Israeli occupation and the military force used to maintain it. For example, General Dynamics manufactures diesel engines for Israel's battle tanks; General Electric supplies the propulsion system for Israel's assault helicopters; and Motorola has a contract to supply the military with wireless encrypted communications in the West Bank.[9] Borders are selectively porous in empire.

Mark's Jesus forces the disciples to face the chaos. Christians, Jews, and Muslims do so today, working for justice and peace in Palestine and Israel. Jews in the United States and Israel speak, write, and witness for peace with justice: Jewish Voice for Peace, Rabbis for Human Rights, and Bat Shalom, to mention only a few. Some denominations, such as the United Methodists and the Presbyterians, have divestment task forces that monitor and report on companies that profit from the Israeli occupation of Palestine—assisting their members and others to reconcile their religious beliefs on justice and peace with their financial and investment decisions.[10] To the border crossers, Jesus says, "It is I, do not be afraid."

How would you describe today's leadership on a local, state, and national level?

CHAPTER 10

MARK 7 _____

Mark 7:1-23

¹Now when the Pharisees and some of the scribes who had come from Jerusalem gathered around him, ²they noticed that some of his disciples were eating with defiled hands, that is, without washing them. ³(For the Pharisees, and all the Jews, do not eat unless they thoroughly wash their hands, thus observing the tradition of the elders; ⁴and they do not eat anything from the market unless they wash it; and there are also many other traditions that they observe, the washing of cups, pots, and bronze kettles.) ⁵So the Pharisees and the scribes asked him, "Why do your disciples not live according to the tradition of the elders, but eat with defiled hands?" ⁶He said to them, "Isaiah prophesied rightly about you hypocrites, as it is written, 'This people honors me with their lips, but their hearts are far from me; ⁷in vain do they worship me, teaching human precepts as doctrines.' ⁸You abandon the commandment of God and hold to human tradition." ⁹Then he said to them, "You have a fine way of rejecting the commandment of God in order to keep your tradition! ¹⁰For Moses said, 'Honor your father and your mother'; and, 'Whoever speaks evil of father or mother must surely die.' ¹¹But you say that if anyone tells father or mother, 'Whatever support you might have had from me is Corban' (that is, an offering to God)— ¹²then you no longer permit doing anything for a father or mother, ¹³thus making void the word of God through your tradition that you have handed on. And you do many things like this." ¹⁴Then he called the crowd again and said to them, "Listen to me, all of you, and understand: ¹⁵there is nothing outside a person that by going in can defile, but the things that come out are what defile." ¹⁷When

he had left the crowd and entered the house, his disciples asked him about the parable. [18]He said to them, "Then do you also fail to understand? Do you not see that whatever goes into a person from outside cannot defile, [19]since it enters, not the heart but the stomach, and goes out into the sewer?" (Thus he declared all foods clean.) [20]And he said, "It is what comes out of a person that defiles. [21]For it is from within, from the human heart, that evil intentions come: fornication, theft, murder, [22]adultery, avarice, wickedness, deceit, licentiousness, envy, slander, pride, folly. [23]All these evil things come from within, and they defile a person."

The issue here is not hygienic purity, but ritual purity before God, achieved through hand washing proscribed for sacrificial food. The Pharisees are going beyond Torah by demanding that "ordinary food be eaten in a state of purity that otherwise was required only for sacrificial food."[1] Such ritual was a burden on the poor who couldn't afford the time or cost of this ceremonial cleanness. Jesus, however, insists that it is not our external circumstances that determine our relation with God. What is in our heart determines that relation. The practice of *corban,* consecrating or willing one's resources to the Jerusalem temple, meant that personal assets belonged to the temple treasury and, although still in the hands of the owner, could not be used to provide support to one's parents, hence destroying the safety net for the elderly. Jesus indicts the practice of *corban* because it hid economic exploitation behind public piety.

Jesus indicts exploitation of the poor, which occurs on both an individual and a societal basis. In Illustration 10.1, a laborer in Morocco spreads cement to pave a street. At the same time this photo was taken, Morocco was secretly accepting from the CIA terrorist suspects for "enhanced interrogation" in the American "War on Terror." That is, the United States was outsourcing torture to a poor country, an ally in the empire. What is unclean—this laborer, or rendition and "enhanced interrogation"? Today, where do we see the murder, theft, deceit, envy, slander, arrogance, and folly condemned as evil by Jesus? Do we justify any of these sins in the name of empire, as the Romans did two thousand years ago?

10.1 Man spreading cement in Morocco

Mark 7:24-30

²⁴From there he set out and went away to the region of Tyre. He entered a house and did not want anyone to know he was there. Yet he could not escape notice, ²⁵but a woman whose little daughter had an unclean spirit immediately heard about him, and she came and bowed down at his feet. ²⁶Now the woman was a Gentile, of Syrophoenician origin. She begged him to cast the demon out of her daughter. ²⁷He said to her, "Let the children be fed first, for it is not fair to take the children's food and throw it to the dogs." ²⁸But she answered him, "Sir, even the dogs under the table eat the children's crumbs." ²⁹Then he said to her, "For saying that, you may go—the demon has left your daughter." ³⁰So she went home, found the child lying on the bed, and the demon gone.

Jesus has returned to Gentile land, to the northwest of Galilee, for the first time since the people in the Gentile Decapolis begged him to leave after he healed the demoniac.[2] Much has been written of the apparent prejudice of Jesus to Gentiles presented in this story. How does one understand Jesus' put-down of a woman begging for her daughter's life? Some have understood it as an exhausted man's loss of patience and annoyance at being pursued into a house where he had sought rest. David Rhodes theorizes that the Gentile Decapolis' rejection of Jesus may have led him to believe he was not able to minister in Gentile lands, and consequently he rebuffed the Syro-Phoenician woman until she clearly demonstrated her need for and faith in him. Another way to understand Jesus' response is through the honor/shame morality of first-century Palestine. As an honorable man, Jesus was bound to rebuff the advances of a strange woman who pursued him into a house and thereby challenged that honor. However, having established his honor, he healed her daughter.

This woman is the second woman in Mark to reach beyond societal norms, to claim and to receive wholeness. As Schüssler Fiorenza points out, she is a triply outcast person who brazenly crossed boundaries for liberation. Outcast as a single woman in a man's world, outcast as a Greek in a cultural/linguistic world of Aramaic, and outcast as a Syro-Phoenician in the national/racial world of Galilee/Judea Judaism, she nevertheless pursued Jesus and gained liberation for her daughter. Daring to enter the house where he is staying and verbally challenging him to include her and her daughter in his wholeness, this woman is the only character in Mark to outwit Jesus in a discussion or argument. She does so by calling him "Lord" (*kyrios*—master). He is the master in a kyrocentric world in which she as a single, unaccompanied, foreign woman is at the bottom of the pyramid of power.[3]

Schüssler Fiorenza understands this story as a call to "re-vision Christian faith as a combative, argumentative, and emancipator praxis that seeks the well being of all."[4] The Gentile woman gains healing for her daughter, but she had to struggle to get it. Moreover, her winning the argument with Jesus marked a critical new step in the Jesus movement—the acknowledged inclusion of Gentiles in the movement—making visible "women's contribution to one of the most crucial transitions in early Christian beginnings."[5] Schüssler Fiorenza identifies the Syro-Phoenician as the "apostolic 'foremother' of all Gentile Christians."[6] Her tenacious crossing of borders results in Jesus' changing his mind and a new commitment to Gentile ministry, in itself a border crossing. Rhodes likens the reactions of early readers or listeners to Jesus' border crossings to Tyre and the Decapolis to the reactions of modern readers to ministries into Mexico from the United States.[7]

Mark 7:31-37

> [31]Then he returned from the region of Tyre, and went by way of Sidon towards the Sea of Galilee, in the region of the Decapolis. [32]They brought to him a deaf man who had an impediment in his speech; and they begged him to lay his hand on him. [33]He took him aside in private, away from the crowd, and put his fingers into his ears, and he spat and touched his tongue. [34]Then looking up to heaven, he sighed and said to him, "Ephphatha," that is, "Be opened." [35]And immediately his ears were opened, his tongue was released, and he spoke plainly. [36]Then Jesus ordered them to tell no one; but the more he ordered them, the more zealously they proclaimed it. [37]They were astounded beyond measure, saying, "He has done everything well; he even makes the deaf to hear and the mute to speak."

Presumably the healed demoniac, whom Jesus told to go home and share "how much the Lord had done for him," has proclaimed his transformation and liberation, opening the Decapolis for a Gentile ministry similar to the ministry to Jewish people.[8]

CHAPTER 11

MARK 8 _____

Mark 8:1-10

¹In those days when there was again a great crowd without anything to eat, he called his disciples and said to them, ²"I have compassion for the crowd, because they have been with me now for three days and have nothing to eat. ³If I send them away hungry to their homes, they will faint on the way—and some of them have come from a great distance." ⁴His disciples replied, "How can one feed these people with bread here in the desert?" ⁵He asked them, "How many loaves do you have?" They said, "Seven." ⁶Then he ordered the crowd to sit down on the ground; and he took the seven loaves, and after giving thanks he broke them and gave them to his disciples to distribute; and they distributed them to the crowd. ⁷They had also a few small fish; and after blessing them, he ordered that these too should be distributed. ⁸They ate and were filled; and they took up the broken pieces left over, seven baskets full. ⁹Now there were about four thousand people. And he sent them away. ¹⁰And immediately he got into the boat with his disciples and went to the district of Dalmanutha.

This is Jesus' second feeding of the crowds and the second time he takes the bread, gives thanks, and breaks the bread so all may eat. The third time will be with his disciples the night he is betrayed and crucified. When we take communion thinking of that Last Supper, do we remember that Jesus broke bread so that all might eat? In this scene, the disciples still didn't understand. Do we?

Jesus has compassion for the people. "Compassion" comes from the Indo-European root *pei*, which means "to suffer." Jesus says "I suf-

11.1 Tea pickers walking home

fer with these people, who are hungry and will faint on the way home should I send them away."

In this picture from Sri Lanka, tea pickers return home from work on a tea plantation in the setting sun (Illus. 11.1). After twelve hours picking tea, they walk several miles up the mountain to mud-floored, thatched-roofed, one-room homes without electricity or plumbing. Such poverty is the life of most of the rural poor throughout the Two-Thirds World, many of them on fields and plantations growing crops for the United States and Europe: tea, coffee, cocoa, fruits, and vegetables. Such absolute poverty does not have to be. In the ethical trade movement of the last fifteen years, some tea, coffee, and cocoa plantations are providing workers with more just working conditions. We in the First World can choose to purchase goods selectively, seeking products that are produced on plantations or in factories where workers are paid living wages.[1] It is breaking the bread, in Jesus' name, so all may eat.

Mark 8:11-13

[11]The Pharisees came and began to argue with him, asking him for a sign from heaven, to test him. [12]And he sighed deeply in his

spirit and said, "Why does this generation ask for a sign? Truly I tell you, no sign will be given to this generation." [13]And he left them, and getting into the boat again, he went across to the other side.

The Pharisees are demanding a sign from God in the manner of the Hebrew Testament prophets that would confirm the authority of Jesus. Although we understand the symbols of the realm to be healing, feeding, and restoration to wholeness, in Mark such miracles are the result of faith rather than signs to prompt faith. In Mark, a sign is "associated with claims and actions of false prophets"; hence, Jesus refuses.[2]

Mark 8:14-21

[14]Now the disciples had forgotten to bring any bread; and they had only one loaf with them in the boat. [15]And he cautioned them, saying, "Watch out—beware of the yeast of the Pharisees and the yeast of Herod." [16]They said to one another, "It is because we have no bread." [17]And becoming aware of it, Jesus said to them, "Why are you talking about having no bread? Do you still not perceive or understand? Are your hearts hardened? [18]Do you have eyes, and fail to see? Do you have ears, and fail to hear? And do you not remember? [19]When I broke the five loaves for the five thousand, how many baskets full of broken pieces did you collect?" They said to him, "Twelve." [20]"And the seven for the four thousand, how many baskets full of broken pieces did you collect?" And they said to him, "Seven." [21]Then he said to them, "Do you not yet understand?"

The disciples struggle to be compassionate in their world. Jesus declares that they just don't get it! Jesus speaks using the metaphor of the yeast of the Pharisees and Herod—yeast, as a small hidden thing that causes bread to rise, yet, it can also be "a symbol of corruption because it can cause bread to become stale or moldy."[3] The disciples don't understand. Their eyes remain blind and their ears remain unhearing. Jesus' exasperation is plain.

Today in a similar way, many Americans struggle with how to respond in the face of global poverty. I am reminded of when my family and I lived in Bolivia following disastrous crop failures of potatoes, rice, and wheat in 1983; there was scarcity and hoarding of foodstuffs. At night, poor people slipped over the five-foot-high walls that surrounded our house and other houses in the neighborhood to steal the garbage cans and eat the garbage in them. In time, massive American shipments of food aid, many provided by American nonprofit organizations, including the one I worked for, eased the food scarcity and communal action to expose food speculators' wholesale hoarding of food brought more food into the markets. Distribution rather than scarcity is the long-term problem. Jesus said, "Do you not yet understand?"

Ten years to the day after editorials in the Kenyan newspapers about 9/11, American newspapers recounted a tragedy in Kenya. Over 120 people had been killed; many more were horribly burnt and hundreds of shanty dwellings went up in flames. A gas pipeline under a Nairobi slum had burst. The slum was an illegal settlement where the homeless and destitute had built densely packed shanties over vacant land and around an open city sewer. For several years, the city government and gas company had ordered the people to dismantle their huts and evacuate the area. But, there was nowhere for these absolutely poor people, most of them rural migrants to the city in search of jobs, to go. When the gas leak was noticed to be spilling gas into the sewer, rather than fleeing it, in their dire poverty people ran to the leak with every container they could round up to collect the gas and sell it. The wind shifted, the gas exploded, and in the words of the vice president of Kenya, "These people died like goats."[4]

On this abundant planet, the world's inequity and desperate poverty cannot be seen as anything but sinful. Jesus tells his disciples to do something about it. Every denomination has ways for Christians to be involved in eliminating global poverty.

Mark 8:22-26

[22]They came to Bethsaida. Some people brought a blind man to him and begged him to touch him. [23]He took the blind man by the hand and led him out of the village; and when he had put saliva on his eyes and laid his hands on him, he asked him, "Can

you see anything?" ²⁴And the man looked up and said, "I can see people, but they look like trees, walking." ²⁵Then Jesus laid his hands on his eyes again; and he looked intently and his sight was restored, and he saw everything clearly. ²⁶Then he sent him away to his home, saying, "Do not even go into the village."

This story is a "call" story like the story of the paralytic man in Mark's second chapter, and it is similar to the healing of the deaf-mute (7:31-37) as well as to the upcoming healing of blind Bartimaeus at the end of the journey to Jerusalem (10:46-52). Jesus invites both men to follow him and enter the realm of God. The healing ritual of the deaf-mute and the Bethsaida blind man are the same, and are similar to Gentile stories of healing miracles. However, all these stories reverberate with and are based on the Hebrew prophets' vision of an alternative world of justice and peace that God will bring about and in which God will reign. The prophet Isaiah says, "Then will the eyes of the blind be opened and the ears of the deaf unstopped. Then will the lame leap like a deer and the mute tongue shout for joy" (Isa. 35:5-6.) In that time, the poor will not dig through garbage cans for something to eat, and the destitute will not need to build upon gas lines and along open city sewers.

Perceiving the realm of God within our midst is a process of understanding ourselves within the social, political, and economic context of our lives, whether we live along open city sewers, in rural or urban poverty, or suburban or urban comfort. Jesus as teacher and healer enables those with eyes to see to understand and act upon the reality of their lives. Sight, understanding, and action don't come all at once. Isn't that the way faith is for many of us? We catch a glimpse of the realm of God—but then it is gone, or we are confused, or we are conflicted by the demands of discipleship. The second time Jesus lays his hands on the blind man, the man "looks intently" and then sees everything clearly. For the disciples, the struggle to see clearly will continue throughout the journey to Jerusalem. The recovery of sight of Bartimaeus will conclude the journey to Jerusalem even as the gradual healing of the Bethsaida man begins it. Gradually, the disciples are learning to see.

Mark 8:27–9:1

²⁷Jesus went on with his disciples to the villages of Caesarea Philippi; and on the way he asked his disciples, "Who do people say that I am?" ²⁸And they answered him, "John the Baptist; and others, Elijah; and still others, one of the prophets." ²⁹He asked them, "But who do you say that I am?" Peter answered him, "You are the Messiah." ³⁰And he sternly ordered them not to tell anyone about him. ³¹Then he began to teach them that the Son of Man must undergo great suffering, and be rejected by the elders, the chief priests, and the scribes, and be killed, and after three days rise again. ³²He said all this quite openly. And Peter took him aside and began to rebuke him. ³³But turning and looking at his disciples, he rebuked Peter and said, "Get behind me, Satan! For you are setting your mind not on divine things but on human things." ³⁴He called the crowd with his disciples, and said to them, "If any want to become my followers, let them deny themselves and take up their cross and follow me. ³⁵For those who want to save their life will lose it, and those who lose their life for my sake, and for the sake of the gospel, will save it. ³⁶For what will it profit them to gain the whole world and forfeit their life? ³⁷Indeed, what can they give in return for their life? ³⁸Those who are ashamed of me and of my words in this adulterous and sinful generation, of them the Son of Man will also be ashamed when he comes in the glory of his Father with the holy angels." ⁹·¹And he said to them, "Truly I tell you, there are some standing here who will not taste death until they see that the kingdom of God has come with power."

Recognition is the theme of this passage. Peter declares that Jesus is the Messiah outside Caesarea Philippi, one of the great cities of the Decapolis. The city had previously been called Paneas because of its worship of the Greek god Pan. In Jesus' day, travelers could worship statues of Pan in niches carved into the rock-wall sides of the road. Herod the Great's son, Philip, renamed it Caesarea in honor of Caesar Augustus. A temple to Augustus accompanied the renaming, rebuilding, and glorification of the city. Sean Freyne, describing the new temples to "Roma and Augustus" in Caesarea Philippi and other nearby cities, quotes the Roman propaganda of Virgil: "their empire would know no bounds, nor periods, dominion without end."[5] It is outside this imperial city, with its new temple to Caesar, that Peter will proclaim that Jesus is the Messiah, the long-awaited king who would liberate Israel.

In the first century the Hebrew word "messiah" (translated into Greek as "Christ") meant "anointed," as a king would be anointed. Hope and expectation for such a kingly leader were biblically based; the messiah would bring justice and peace to a liberated Israel after generations of occupation, exploitation, and oppression. The prophets Jeremiah (Jer. 23:5-6), Micah (Mic. 5:2), and Isaiah (Isa. 11:2-9) spoke of their hopes for such a leader. Isaiah's imagery is particularly familiar and beloved today.

> The spirit of the Lord shall rest on him, the spirit of wisdom and understanding, the spirit of counsel and might, the spirit of knowledge and the fear of the Lord. His delight shall be in the fear of the Lord. He shall not judge by what his eyes see, or decide by what his ears hear; but with righteousness he shall judge the poor, and decide with equity for the meek of the earth; he shall strike the earth with the rod of his mouth, and with the breath of his lips he shall kill the wicked. Righteousness shall be the belt around his waist, and faithfulness the belt around his loins. The wolf shall live with the lamb, the leopard shall lie down with the kid, the calf and the lion and the fatling together, and a little child shall lead them. The cow and the bear shall graze, their young shall lie down together; and the lion shall eat straw like the ox. The nursing child shall play over the hole of the asp, and the weaned child shall put its hand on the adder's den. They will not hurt or destroy on all my holy mountain; for the earth will be full of the knowledge of the Lord as the waters cover the sea. (Isa. 11:2-9)

Although all messianic expectation was communal and centered on Israel, there was not a uniform expectation of the messiah in the decades before Jesus' ministry. The book of Daniel and first-century writings (for example, scrolls from the caves of Qumran, the *Parables of Enoch,* and the *Psalms of Solomon)* that did not make the Hebrew canon illustrate some of the hope and diverse thinking of that troubled time.[6] The *Parables of Enoch,* evoking Daniel, present a militant Son of Man who will establish righteousness and be a "light of the nations." The *Psalms of Solomon,* presenting hope for a messiah who will deliver Jerusalem from the Romans, contains language that is both violent and nonviolent.

Jesus understands Peter's acclamation of him as a kingly, militant messiah and firmly rejects the idea. Jesus as a suffering Son of Man will be different. Contrary to expectations of messianic redemptive violence and unlike the Galilean challengers and messianic rebels against the occupation and oppression of empire in Palestine with whom the Markan community would have been familiar, Jesus' resistance will be nonviolent. Jesus' challenge, however, was a political call from an imperial city in the face of Caesar, Roman occupation and oppression, and the knowledge that Rome tortured and executed those who dared to defy the empire. Identified by Peter as the Messiah, Jesus responds with the first of three predictions of his suffering and crucifixion.

We so often domesticate the expression of bearing one's cross to refer to daily burdens or long-term burdens of illness, brokenness, or pain. There is no such domestication here, but a call to suffering, nonviolent resistance, trusting in God and God's eternal goodness, justice, and love. Jesus makes it clear that we are called to be faithful, wherever that may lead us. To be saved is not to be safe; it is to be made whole, as the demoniac in the tombs and the hemorrhaging woman were made whole. The word "save" comes from the Indo-European root *sol,* which means "whole." To be saved is to be made whole.

Discipleship is a journey. Jesus describes "the Way" as he travels with his disciples from northern Palestine to the outskirts of Jerusalem. He gives them three key lessons: "whosoever would save his life will lose it"; "if anyone would be first, he must be last"; and "whosoever would be great among you must be your servant." These lessons, born out of the first-century Mediterranean patriarchal world's preoccupation with honor and shame, challenge the domination and pride of the powerful. They are addressed to the male disciples who argue with Jesus for his refusal to assume a militant messiah role and who battle among themselves for dominance as his followers.

In these lessons, Mark presents Jesus as a man challenging the standards of honor and shame of his day and crossing the borders of his culture. The "boundary markers" of honor, which was "a claim to worth along with the social acknowledgement of that worth" were authority, gender status and respect.[7] Male honor stood on "manliness, courage, authority over family, willingness to defend one's reputation, and refusal to submit to humiliation." Female honor rested on "sensitivity about one's own reputation, sensitivity to the opinions of others,"[8] who demanded subordinate, secluded, and timid behavior of women. In lessons that emphasize taking a subordinate and losing position, Jesus is negating the claims of authority, demands for respect, and gender privilege of traditional male honor.

We must interpret Mark's lessons on servanthood with care, in light of privileges of nationality, ethnicity, class, race, and gender. For centuries, the powerful and dominant have used such lessons to justify the servanthood and subordination of the vulnerable and subordinate—blacks during slavery and women during all periods—further exploiting the exploited. In Mark, however, these lessons are not addressed to the vulnerable, the disenfranchised, the ill, or to women, who were already of subordinate and restricted social status. Jesus addresses them to his dominant, status-seeking male disciples.

Salvation for these barefoot Bangladeshi women is not a call to be the least, the last, and a servant (Illus. 11.2). They already are. Hauling water for their families' drinking, cooking, and bathing, they live in the capital city of one of the poorest countries in the world where factories filled largely with teenage girls produce clothing and shoes for the American market. While living in Bangladesh in 1996/1997, I passed hundreds of their sisters each morning on their way to those factories where worker safety, rights, and payment were minimized to meet American and European demand for inexpensive clothing. Full-time workers earned as little as US$40 a month; compulsory overtime was common and usually uncompensated. In November 2012, a horrific fire in the Tarzeen apparel factory killed 122 workers and exposed to international view American corporate collusion in the systemic exploitation of the Bangladesh apparel industry.

The empire of Caesar is both an old and a modern story about an affluent global center and the poor periphery. We wear clothes made

11.2 Bangladeshi
women at water tap

in Bangladesh factories, not realizing that many of the workers labor
under terrible conditions to produce that clothing. Enslaved Indians
labored and died in the silver mines of Potosi of colonial Bolivia, yielding the fabulous wealth to fuel the industrial revolution of Europe.
Enslaved Indian labor in Iquitos, Peru, and in vast areas of the Amazon
was the basis for the nineteenth- and twentieth-century's rubber boom,
providing rubber tires for the United States' new automobile industry.
In today's Brazilian Amazon, multinational demand for beef and soy
and Brazilian demand for foreign exchange underlie the expansion
of agribusiness into the rainforest where Indian and slave-descendant
communities struggle to maintain their land.

Mark's apocalyptic literature, which concluded the lessons on discipleship, opens our eyes to an alternative: the kingdom of God. Such literature enables us to see through the propaganda, standards, and rules
of this world to the world God wills. Two realms actually co-exist; we
need only eyes to see them both.[9] Mark declares there is the empire

of Caesar, proclaimed as a god, who arrives in shining armament with the empire's power beside him. There is the realm of Jesus' Father, the liberating God of justice and peace, who has "holy angels" for accompaniment.

Sister Dorothy Stang, S.N.D., a Catholic nun from Ohio, is an example of those with eyes to see and choose between the empire of Caesar and the kingdom of God. Her discipleship journey led to twenty years working for human rights in a region of slave labor, rancher aggression, illegal logging, and violent land conflicts in the Brazilian Amazon. At her death in 2005 she was working under the Pastoral Land Commission with slave-descendant communities, *Quilombos*, caught in conflict with loggers and ranchers who wanted *Quilombo* land for agribusiness and were willing to kill for it. In the Pastoral Land Commission, an ecumenical organization founded by the National Conference of Brazilian Bishops, the church stood with the disenfranchised to promote social justice and land reform for those exploited by generations of empire. *Christianity Today* described Sister Dorothy's death:

> Despite her passion and sacrifices for the people, she received countless death threats over the years for her advocacy work. Reported by Associated Press, the murder took place when Stang was on her way to a meeting with local activists about land reform last weekend. Two gunmen approached her; a witness said Stang pulled the Bible from her bag when she was confronted and started reading. Her killers listened for a moment, took a few steps back and fired. They shot her three times in the face, the police said.[10]

How do we who are privileged understand Mark's discipleship lessons on a global level? In Jesus' message about discipleship outside Caesarea Philippi, he critiques this "adulterous and sinful generation"—in the tradition of the Hebrew Testament that likened Israel's idolatry and adoption of foreign gods to adultery. The disciples must make a choice. Which realm or kingdom will we serve?

CHAPTER 12

MARK 9 _____

Mark 9:2-13

²Six days later, Jesus took with him Peter and James and John, and led them up a high mountain apart, by themselves. And he was transfigured before them, ³and his clothes became dazzling white, such as no one on earth could bleach them. ⁴And there appeared to them Elijah with Moses, who were talking with Jesus. ⁵Then Peter said to Jesus, "Rabbi, it is good for us to be here; let us make three dwellings, one for you, one for Moses, and one for Elijah." ⁶He did not know what to say, for they were terrified. ⁷Then a cloud overshadowed them, and from the cloud there came a voice, "This is my Son, the Beloved; listen to him!" ⁸Suddenly when they looked around, they saw no one with them any more, but only Jesus. ⁹As they were coming down the mountain, he ordered them to tell no one about what they had seen, until after the Son of Man had risen from the dead. ¹⁰So they kept the matter to themselves, questioning what this rising from the dead could mean. ¹¹Then they asked him, "Why do the scribes say that Elijah must come first?" ¹²He said to them, "Elijah is indeed coming first to restore all things. How then is it written about the Son of Man, that he is to go through many sufferings and be treated with contempt? ¹³But I tell you that Elijah has come, and they did to him whatever they pleased, as it is written about him."

The journey continues with flashes of insight followed by bumbling blindness. High on the peace and quiet of a mountain, the disciples are able to see Jesus clearly in dazzling white clothes, the apocalyptic symbol of martyrdom. In their eyes, he is firmly within the tradition of the Jewish messiah, talking with Elijah, who represents prophetic vision, and Moses, who represents the Torah, or Law. Peter tries to hold on to the moment by building something physical. Is that what we disciples do when we are afraid? Seek refuge in an institution?

Although the entire Gospel is about the nature of God as experienced in the person of Jesus, God appears or speaks in only a few veiled instances. The voice behind the cloud presumably is God's, and the scene reminds us of God speaking during Jesus' baptism. In both scenes, Jesus is God's beloved son. The first scene, at the beginning of Jesus' ministry, and this second scene, at the beginning of the journey to the cross, "point forward to the centurion's identification of Jesus at his death on the cross: 'Truly this man was the son of God.'"[1] God says, "Listen to him!" Listen to Jesus on this final stage of the discipleship journey and learn about the realm of God. In the context of Roman occupation and oppression, Jesus will live out and teach the liberation from injustice, domination, and misery that Moses and the prophets promised for God's faithful people. As he walks to Jerusalem and his cross, Jesus will turn societal expectations about domination and subordination on their heads. But it is only when the disciples have understood Jesus' passion predictions, after the crucifixion and the empty tomb, that questions and answers about the greatest and the least, insiders and outsiders, males and females, children and adults, rich and poor, can be truly understood.

Mark 9:14-29

[14]When they came to the disciples, they saw a great crowd around them, and some scribes arguing with them. [15]When the whole crowd saw him, they were immediately overcome with awe, and they ran forward to greet him. [16]He asked them, "What are you arguing about with them?" [17]Someone from the crowd answered him, "Teacher, I brought you my son; he has a spirit that makes him unable to speak; [18]and whenever it seizes him, it dashes him down; and he foams and grinds his teeth and becomes rigid; and I asked your disciples to cast it out, but they could not do so." [19]He answered them, "You faithless generation, how much longer must I be among you? How much longer must I put up with you? Bring him to me." [20]And they brought the

boy to him. When the spirit saw him, immediately it convulsed the boy, and he fell on the ground and rolled about, foaming at the mouth. ²¹Jesus asked the father, "How long has this been happening to him?" And he said, "From childhood. ²²It has often cast him into the fire and into the water, to destroy him; but if you are able to do anything, have pity on us and help us." ²³Jesus said to him, "If you are able! —All things can be done for the one who believes." ²⁴Immediately the father of the child cried out, "I believe; help my unbelief!" ²⁵When Jesus saw that a crowd came running together, he rebuked the unclean spirit, saying to it, "You spirit that keeps this boy from speaking and hearing, I command you, come out of him, and never enter him again!" ²⁶After crying out and convulsing him terribly, it came out, and the boy was like a corpse, so that most of them said, "He is dead." ²⁷But Jesus took him by the hand and lifted him up, and he was able to stand. ²⁸When he had entered the house, his disciples asked him privately, "Why could we not cast it out?" ²⁹He said to them, "This kind can come out only through prayer."

The ministry of Jesus is a struggle between the goodness of God and evil, represented here as an evil spirit who left a boy helpless and dashed upon the ground. Is that boy a metaphor for the Jewish people as they lived under Rome's occupation and exploitation—dashed to the ground and hopeless? Is he a metaphor for us during times of trial and testing—when faith seems as dry and illusive as fall leaves in a gale-force wind? The father's outcry, "I believe; help my unbelief!" captures many believers of all generations, suspended between fear and faith at some critical point in their lives. Many of us have cried out with just such sentiments—hoping for the courage of faith to say "yes" to the discipleship journey ahead of us.

Jesus urges prayer. Myers notes that Jesus invites his disciples to pray on just two other occasions. One is his temple action, "when he urges the disciples to believe in the possibility of a world free of the exploitive temple-state. . . . The other is just before Jesus is seized by security forces, when he summons his followers to prayer as a way of 'staying awake' to the Way of the cross. . . . The powers rule in our heart and in the world through the despair that persuades us that genuine personal and social transformation is impossible, and we have been socialized into such resignation 'from childhood.' To pray is to re-center our consciousness around a faith that insists on the possibility and imperative of such transformation."[2]

Mark 9:30-41

[30]They went on from there and passed through Galilee. He did not want anyone to know it; [31]for he was teaching his disciples, saying to them, "The Son of Man is to be betrayed into human hands, and they will kill him, and three days after being killed, he will rise again." [32]But they did not understand what he was saying and were afraid to ask him. [33]Then they came to Capernaum; and when he was in the house he asked them, "What were you arguing about on the way?" [34]But they were silent, for on the way they had argued with one another who was the greatest. [35]He sat down, called the twelve, and said to them, "Whoever wants to be first must be last of all and servant of all." [36]Then he took a little child and put it among them; and taking it in his arms, he said to them, [37]"Whoever welcomes one such child in my name welcomes me, and whoever welcomes me welcomes not me but the one who sent me." [38]John said to him, "Teacher, we saw someone casting out demons in your name, and we tried to stop him, because he was not following us." [39]But Jesus said, "Do not stop him; for no one who does a deed of power in my name will be able soon afterward to speak evil of me. [40]Whoever is not against us is for us. [41]For truly I tell you, whoever gives you a cup of water to drink because you bear the name of Christ will by no means lose the reward.

Jesus is trying to have some quality time with his disciples, while there is still time; he wants them to understand the meaning of his ministry and his anticipated death at the hands of the Romans and the collaborating Jewish elites. It is an explicit prediction of his death and resurrection; but the disciples don't understand, and they don't dare to ask questions. He is the teacher—but they don't dare to be learners.

Like so much of their world and ours, the disciples are obsessed with domination and subordination, status and honor, who belongs and

12.1 Bolivian children begging

who doesn't belong in their hierarchical world. Earlier they quarreled over who would sit at Jesus' right hand; now they argue over who is the greatest. The stories of these two children, the possessed boy and the embraced child, illustrate both the disciples continued blindness and the nature of the realm of God. Jesus embraces those at the very bottom of the social order. While our Sunday School pictures portray Jesus welcoming well-scrubbed children, the condition of most children in his time—as it is for many small children now—is that they are vulnerable, hungry, dirty, and hard at work at an early age, like these Bolivian children begging for bread (Illus. 12.1). When I took the picture in 1983, a common expression of poor Bolivians, used to small children given the job of tending the sheep or taking care of even smaller children, was, "Everyone five and over has to earn their daily bread." What would we do if we were to welcome one of these children in Jesus' name?

Mark 9:42-50

⁴²"If any of you put a stumbling block before one of these little ones who believe in me, it would be better for you if a great

millstone were hung around your neck and you were thrown into the sea. [43]If your hand causes you to stumble, cut it off; it is better for you to enter life maimed than to have two hands and to go to hell, to the unquenchable fire. [45]And if your foot causes you to stumble, cut it off; it is better for you to enter life lame than to have two feet and to be thrown into hell. [47]And if your eye causes you to stumble, tear it out; it is better for you to enter the kingdom of God with one eye than to have two eyes and to be thrown into hell, [48]where their worm never dies, and the fire is never quenched. [49]"For everyone will be salted with fire. [50]Salt is good; but if salt has lost its saltiness, how can you season it? Have salt in yourselves, and be at peace with one another."

Mark is stressing that those who follow Jesus will have to make painful sacrifices. Jesus is not advocating self-mutilation, however; our hands symbolize what we do, our feet the journey we take, and our eyes what we see. Discipleship is how we live; the choices we make and the decisions we make or fail to make. Mark contrasts the results of those choices and decisions: the realm of God or "hell," a translation of "Gehenna," the valley of Hinnom southwest of Jerusalem, which was associated with the pagan worship of the god Moloch and the sacrifice of children by fire on altars. The images of worms that never die and fire that is never quenched come from the concluding chapter of Isaiah, in which Isaiah describes the Lord's final judgment and creation of a new heaven and a new earth. This intensifies the gravity of faithful decision making. Fire links the sayings on decision making and judgment with those on salt, which in the Hebrew Testament is used to purify, as a sacrifice, and in covenants. Mark concludes, urging that "Jesus' disciples cultivate hospitality and peace."[3]

CHAPTER 13

MARK 10 _____

Mark 10:1-16

¹He left that place and went to the region of Judea and beyond the Jordan. And crowds again gathered around him; and, as was his custom, he again taught them. ²Some Pharisees came, and to test him they asked, "Is it lawful for a man to divorce his wife?" ³He answered them, "What did Moses command you?" ⁴They said, "Moses allowed a man to write a certificate of dismissal and to divorce her." ⁵But Jesus said to them, "Because of your hardness of heart he wrote this commandment for you. ⁶But from the beginning of creation, 'God made them male and female.' ⁷For this reason a man shall leave his father and mother and be joined to his wife, ⁸and the two shall become one flesh.' So they are no longer two, but one flesh. ⁹Therefore what God has joined together, let no one separate." ¹⁰Then in the house the disciples asked him again about this matter. ¹¹He said to them, "Whoever divorces his wife and marries another commits adultery against her; ¹²and if she divorces her husband and marries another, she commits adultery." ¹³People were bringing little children to him in order that he might touch them; and the disciples spoke sternly to them. ¹⁴But when Jesus saw this, he was indignant and said to them, "Let the little children come to me; do not stop them; for it is to such as these that the kingdom of God belongs. ¹⁵Truly I tell you, whoever does not receive the kingdom of God as a little child will never enter it." ¹⁶And he took them up in his arms, laid his hands on them, and blessed them.

The Pharisees again attempt to trap Jesus in an honor/shame challenge by questioning his Torah orthodoxy. He turns the question back

upon them and thereby exposes their "hardness of heart." Deuteronomy 24:1, Jewish law on divorce, said a man could divorce his wife if
he found something objectionable in her; a woman could not divorce
her husband. Jesus challenges the inequity of the relationship and the
patriarchal practice of divorce that made women vulnerable and subordinate. The divorce of Persian Queen Vashti in the third-century
B.C.E. Hebrew story of Esther in the Persian court is a good example of
the male hardness of heart that Jesus rejected. Although traditionally
Esther is the heroine in this story, meant to praise fidelity to Jewish
identity, read the story (Esth. 1:1-22) instead with an ear to the power
of patriarchy's deciding the proper role of women. Set in a culture
where women's honor depended upon being secluded from the sight
of all men except immediate family and their husbands, Queen Vashti
is divorced because she refuses to obey the drunken command of her
husband, the king, to display herself before a drunken crowd of noble
men at a royal banquet. The issue is women as property.

Elisabeth Schüssler Fiorenza understands the Markan verses as
Jesus' rejection of patriarchy and writes, "Mark 10:2-9 must be inter-
preted not only as separate from the saying on divorce in 10:10-12 but
not even in light of it."[1]

> The question put before Jesus is totally androcentric (can a
> man dismiss his wife) and presupposes patriarchal marriage as a
> "given." The first exchange between Jesus and the Pharisees makes
> it clear that divorce is necessary because of the male's "hardness
> of heart," that is, because of men's patriarchal mind-set and real-
> ity. As long as patriarchy is operative, divorce is commanded
> out of necessity.... However, Jesus insists, God did not create
> or intend patriarchy but created persons as male and female
> human beings.... The passage is best translated as "the two per-
> sons—man and woman—enter into a common human life and
> social relationships because they are created as equals." The text
> does not refer to the myth of an androgynous primal man but
> to the equal partnership of man and woman in human marriage
> intended and made possible by the creator God. What, therefore,
> God has joined together in equal partnership ..., a human being
> should not separate.[2]

Although adultery was understood to be an offense committed against a man, whose property rights over a woman were violated, and not as a moral offense against women, Jesus negates that understanding with his statement that a man who divorced his wife and married another woman committed adultery against his first wife. Although only men could initiate a divorce, Jesus expands that right to include women and "thereby directly *contradicted* Jewish law, which stipulated that only men could initiate and administer such proceedings."[3]

Two thousand years ago, Jesus critiqued divorce in terms of male hardness of heart. Today, although women have more marital rights, patriarchy and hardness of heart continue to lead to suffering in intimate partner relationships. Domestic abuse and society's tacit acceptance of it are modern equivalents of hardened hearts.

Mark 10:17-31

[17]As he was setting out on a journey, a man ran up and knelt before him, and asked him, "Good Teacher, what must I do to inherit eternal life?" [18]Jesus said to him, "Why do you call me good? No one is good but God alone. [19]You know the commandments: 'You shall not murder; You shall not commit adultery; You shall not steal; You shall not bear false witness; You shall not defraud; Honor your father and mother.'" [20]He said to him, "Teacher, I have kept all these since my youth." [21]Jesus, looking at him, loved him and said, "You lack one thing; go, sell what you own, and give the money to the poor, and you will have treasure in heaven; then come, follow me." [22]When he heard this, he was shocked and went away grieving, for he had many possessions. [23]Then Jesus looked around and said to his disciples, "How hard it will be for those who have wealth to enter the kingdom of God!" [24]And the disciples were perplexed at these words. But Jesus said to them again, "Children, how hard it is to enter the kingdom of God! [25]It is easier for a camel to go through the eye of a needle than for someone who is rich to enter the kingdom of God." [26]They were greatly astounded and said to one another, "Then who can be saved?" [27]Jesus looked at them and said, "For mortals it is impossible, but not for God; for God all things are

possible." [28]Peter began to say to him, "Look, we have left everything and followed you." [29]Jesus said, "Truly I tell you, there is no
one who has left house or brothers or sisters or mother or father
or children or fields, for my sake and for the sake of the good
news, [30]who will not receive a hundredfold now in this age—
houses, brothers and sisters, mothers and children, and fields
with persecutions—and in the age to come eternal life. [31]But
many who are first will be last, and the last will be first."

The story of the rich man, following the story of male hardness
of heart and the vulnerability of children, broadens Jesus' critique of
hardness of heart. The NRSV translation of the man's impediment
is "possessions"; a translation closer to the original Greek is "acquisitions."[4] Two thousand years ago, a person's wealth consisted of their
land. A man with many acquisitions had likely acquired peasant land
lost to debt. His hardness of heart lay in disregarding the Torah commandments on debt and disregarding the lives broken by loss of their
land. As Lamar Williamson notes, it is "essentially a call story. It is the
only such story in Mark in which the person called responds not by
following, but by going away."[5]

Many Christians struggle with this text. How poor do we have to be
to be faithful? How rich can we be and still be faithful? Recent research
indicates that national and global wealth inequality is at historic highs,
that most Americans ideally prefer more equitable distribution and
that they are not aware of the extent of current American inequality.
Today, the richest 1 percent of Americans hold nearly one-third of the
wealth, equaling the levels seen just before the Great Depression in the
1920s. Indeed, the wealthiest 20 percent (quintile) of Americans own
83 percent of American wealth; the poorest 40 percent of American
households own 1 percent.[6] Globally, 40 percent of people (2.7 billion
people) live on less than $2 a day; 24 percent live on less than $1 a day.
Electric refrigerators, hot showers, and clean drinking water, basics that
even poor Americans regard as essentials, are the possessions of only
the privileged few in many countries. As global citizens, most of us are
the rich man in this story. How then do we follow Jesus?

Examining our hearts as Jesus asked of the rich man is the first step.
There are some excellent faith-based tools for looking at faith and eco-

nomics and for acting for justice, the second step, as individuals and as communities of faith. We have examples of disciples, such as Martin Luther King, Jr., who did follow Jesus' call for justice wherever the call led them. He wrote from a jail in Birmingham a timeless message on discipleship.

> I am in Birmingham because injustice is here. Just as the prophets of the eighth century B.C. left their villages and carried their "thus saith the Lord" far beyond the boundaries of their home towns, and just as the Apostle Paul left his village of Tarsus and carried the gospel of Jesus Christ to the far corners of the Greco-Roman world, so am I compelled to carry the gospel of freedom beyond my own home town. Like Paul, I must constantly respond to the Macedonian call for aid. Moreover, I am cognizant of the inter-relatedness of all communities and states. I cannot sit idly by in Atlanta and not be concerned about what happens in Birmingham. Injustice anywhere is a threat to justice everywhere. We are caught in an inescapable network of mutuality, tied in a single garment of destiny. Whatever affects one directly, affects all indirectly.[7]

Some years ago in the Ecuadoran Andes, I met a mother and her two daughters setting out for a journey, walking in homemade leather boots across rugged terrain, to a newly constructed school in a town several miles from their one-room home with no heat, plumbing, or electricity. The mother had never been to school, and the girls were thrilled that on this, their first day, they would be able to learn to read and write. Over and over they said to me, *escuela, escuela*; "school, school" (Illus. 13.1).

School meant new life. It would be a new life enabled by American charitable giving. I don't know if the many donors for that school gave out of their wealth or their poverty, but they are the flip side of Mark's story, a story of ethical choices in a world of "many possessions" and crying human need. Enabling new life for children they would never meet was more important than whatever additional possession or acquisition they might pursue.

In the midst of the story about wealth, Mark places Jesus' reminder that in all times we walk with God. Jesus looked at them and said, "For

13.1 Ecuadoran mother and girls

mortals it is impossible, but not for God; for God all things are possible." God calls us to be faithful; the results are in God's hands.

Mark 10:32-45

[32]They were on the road, going up to Jerusalem, and Jesus was walking ahead of them; they were amazed, and those who followed were afraid. He took the twelve aside again and began to tell them what was to happen to him, [33]saying, "See, we are going up to Jerusalem, and the Son of Man will be handed over to the chief priests and the scribes, and they will condemn him to death; then they will hand him over to the Gentiles; [34]they will mock him, and spit upon him, and flog him, and kill him; and after three days he will rise again." [35]James and John, the sons of Zebedee, came forward to him and said to him, "Teacher, we want you to do for us whatever we ask of you." [36]And he said to them, "What is it you want me to do for you?" [37]And they said to him, "Grant us to sit, one at your right hand and one at your

left, in your glory." [38]But Jesus said to them, "You do not know what you are asking. Are you able to drink the cup that I drink, or be baptized with the baptism that I am baptized with?" [39]They replied, "We are able." Then Jesus said to them, "The cup that I drink you will drink; and with the baptism with which I am baptized, you will be baptized; [40]but to sit at my right hand or at my left is not mine to grant, but it is for those for whom it has been prepared." [41]When the ten heard this, they began to be angry with James and John. [42]So Jesus called them and said to them, "You know that among the Gentiles those whom they recognize as their rulers lord it over them, and their great ones are tyrants over them. [43]But it is not so among you; but whoever wishes to become great among you must be your servant, [44]and whoever wishes to be first among you must be slave of all. [45]For the Son of Man did not come to be served but to serve and to give his life as a ransom for many."

What a picture! Jesus is "leading the way" to his death. The disciples are "astonished" that he is walking steadily ahead to the cross. They are afraid. Again, he takes them aside to prepare them for Jerusalem; it is the third passion prediction and the fullest of the three. The first (8:31) was an announcement; the second (9:31) includes the prediction of being handed over and betrayal, and the third is a synopsis of the final passion itself. In each, the pattern is the same: the prediction, followed by the disciples' misunderstanding, followed by Jesus' teaching on discipleship. James and John respond with another status-seeking request, and Jesus' response of the metaphor of the cup and baptism negates status and honor. Jesus is asking if the disciples can embrace the life that he is preaching and endure the suffering of the cross that he will endure. The disciples still do not understand what lies ahead.

Surrounded by his male disciples in a patriarchal society, Jesus is portrayed as critiquing the pride of his disciples and urging servanthood instead. Throughout the centuries, the saying on servanthood has been used to edify and curb the pride that diminishes others and to point to a way of life that enables others. The saying, however, has also been a tool in the hands of the powerful for keeping the vulnerable, particularly women and children, slaves, and minorities in their subservient place with a properly submissive attitude. As Mary Potter Engle has written, "Powerlessness as well as power corrupts. Power-lessness corrupts women by tempting us to lose ourselves in others."[8] Feminist theologians have questioned whether pride and/or the desire to lord it over others is a significant sin of women, who are raised to subordinate roles in most societies and who consequently, usually, live in subordinate relationships throughout their lives. Is not the lack of healthy self-esteem and individuation—rather than pride—the more typical female sin? Does the patriarchal church contribute to the abuse of the vulnerable by failing to affirm healthy self-esteem while preaching servanthood?

Richard Horsley writes similarly that Jesus is rejecting the societal patterns of domination and subservience that regulated Mediterranean society, including Palestine. The saying is "dealing not merely or vaguely with rank within a community of disciples but with relations of political domination and subservience . . . the subject under discussion is the governance of the society generally, the whole people of Israel, and not the smaller circle of disciples."[9]

Mark 10:46-52

[46]They came to Jericho. As he and his disciples and a large crowd were leaving Jericho, Bartimaeus son of Timaeus, a blind beggar, was sitting by the roadside. [47]When he heard that it was Jesus of Nazareth, he began to shout out and say, "Jesus, Son of David, have mercy on me!" [48]Many sternly ordered him to be quiet, but he cried out even more loudly, "Son of David, have mercy on me!" [49]Jesus stood still and said, "Call him here." And they called the blind man, saying to him, "Take heart; get up, he is calling you." [50]So throwing off his cloak, he sprang up and came to Jesus. [51]Then Jesus said to him, "What do you want me to do for you?" The blind man said to him, "My teacher, let me see again." [52]Jesus said to him, "Go; your faith has made you well." Immediately he regained his sight and followed him on the way.

Blind Bartimaeus, who insistently calls out for Jesus and will not be shut up, becomes a disciple who follows Jesus to Jerusalem through his faith and perseverance. It is a call story in which Bartimaeus and

Jesus call each other and is a foil to the story of James and John that preceded it. In both stories, Jesus asks, "What do you want me to do for you?" James and John wanted status and honor; Bartimaeus, whose name literally translated from Aramaic means "son of filth," [10] wants to see. He does so because of his faith, which Williamson writes "offers a particularly vivid case study of faith. His crying out to Jesus, even with a less than perfect perception of who Jesus is, his persistent refusal to be silenced, his bold and eager response to Jesus' call . . . and his clear focus on the one thing he wanted most in the world, together with his keen anticipation that Jesus could and would grant it, are the attributes and actions which Jesus calls 'faith.'"[11] Bartimaeus has the same audacity and insistence as the bleeding woman who touched his robe, and the Syrophoenician woman who entered the house he was staying in. Faith is pushy!

CHAPTER 14

MARK 11 ⸻

Mark 11:1-11

¹When they were approaching Jerusalem, at Bethphage and Bethany, near the Mount of Olives, he sent two of his disciples ²and said to them, "Go into the village ahead of you, and immediately as you enter it, you will find tied there a colt that has never been ridden; untie it and bring it. ³If anyone says to you, 'Why are you doing this?' just say this, 'The Lord needs it and will send it back here immediately.'" ⁴They went away and found a colt tied near a door, outside in the street. As they were untying it, ⁵some of the bystanders said to them, "What are you doing, untying the colt?" ⁶They told them what Jesus had said; and they allowed them to take it. ⁷Then they brought the colt to Jesus and threw their cloaks on it; and he sat on it. ⁸Many people spread their cloaks on the road, and others spread leafy branches that they had cut in the fields. ⁹Then those who went ahead and those who followed were shouting. "Hosanna! Blessed is the one who comes in the name of the Lord!" ¹⁰Blessed is the coming kingdom of our ancestor David! Hosanna in the highest heaven!" ¹¹Then he entered Jerusalem and went into the temple; and when he had looked around at everything, as it was already late, he went out to Bethany with the twelve.

Jesus' entry into Jerusalem on the first day of Passover is a staged, symbolic protest with prophetic, royal, and messianic images. In Williamson's words, it is "an enthronement procession."[1] Passover was the great annual pilgrimage feast commemorating the Jews' liberation from slavery in Egypt, which eventually brought legendary unity, peace, and prosperity. For seven hundred years, however, except for brief periods of independence, Israel had been a conquered and exploited people. Each Passover celebration of God's action on Israel's behalf stirred hope that God would again lead the people into freedom. Jesus' entry on a colt intentionally enacted the prophet Zechariah's scriptural messianic prophecies: Israel's king would enter Jerusalem lowly and riding on a colt (Zech. 9:9).[2] The people would spread cloaks before him (2 Kgs. 9:13). Shouting "Hosanna! Blessed is the one who comes in the name of the Lord!," the crowds quote Psalm 118:25-26, which pilgrims sang as they approached the temple.

Hosanna means "save us" and was used in addressing kings. In the final judgment of the nations, the Lord would stand on the Mount of Olives, at the edge of the city.[3] While Jesus entered through one gate, the Roman governor Pilate entered from another, with additional troops from his coastal headquarters. The Roman fortress, adjacent to and looking down on the courtyards of the temple, was a permanent symbol of occupation and terror.

Yet as John Donahue and Daniel Harrington note of Jesus' entry, "The kingdom he proclaims and enacts is not that of his ancestor King David, but rather that of his heavenly father. And the decisive event in his activity in Jerusalem will not be some kind of military victory but rather his death on the cross and his resurrection (which represents victory over death)."[4] This royal entry and Jesus' confrontational action in the temple the following day are reasons why Jesus will be crucified as King of the Jews and an enemy of Rome. On his arrival day, Jesus goes to the temple and checks out the situation, but does nothing. The disciples stay with him.

Mark 11:12-25

[12]On the following day, when they came from Bethany, he was hungry. [13]Seeing in the distance a fig tree in leaf, he went to see whether perhaps he would find anything on it. When he came to it, he found nothing but leaves, for it was not the season for figs. [14]He said to it, "May no one ever eat fruit from you again." And his disciples heard it. [15]Then they came to Jerusalem. And he entered the temple and began to drive out those who were selling and those who were buying in the temple, and he overturned the tables of the money changers and the seats of those

who sold doves; [16]and he would not allow anyone to carry anything through the temple. [17]He was teaching and saying, "Is it not written, 'My house shall be called a house of prayer for all the nations'? But you have made it a den of robbers." [18]And when the chief priests and the scribes heard it, they kept looking for a way to kill him; for they were afraid of him, because the whole crowd was spellbound by his teaching. [19]And when evening came, Jesus and his disciples went out of the city. [20]In the morning as they passed by, they saw the fig tree withered away to its roots. [21]Then Peter remembered and said to him, "Rabbi, look! The fig tree that you cursed has withered." [22]Jesus answered them, "Have faith in God. [23]Truly I tell you, if you say to this mountain, 'Be taken up and thrown into the sea,' and if you do not doubt in your heart, but believe that what you say will come to pass, it will be done for you. [24]So I tell you, whatever you ask for in prayer, believe that you have received it, and it will be yours. [25]Whenever you stand praying, forgive, if you have anything against anyone; so that your Father in heaven may also forgive you your trespasses."

Mark has created another "sandwich" here, with two stories of fig trees sandwiching Jesus' action in the temple. The fig tree stories are puzzling. Passover was in April, and Jesus would have known that it was too early for figs to have been ripe. Why then would Jesus, the healer, curse a tree for not bearing fruit out of season? One understanding is that this is a metaphor; the fig tree represents Israel, and its withering represents God's judgment upon temple-based Israel. Micah, the eighth-century B.C.E. prophet of justice, voices such imagery in his critique of the lack of justice in Israel of that day. "Woe is me! For I have become like one who, after the summer fruit has been gathered, after the vintage has been gleaned, finds no cluster to eat; there is no first-ripe fig for which I hunger. The faithful have disappeared from the land, and there is no one left who is upright" (Mic. 7:1-2). Myers writes that the function of the metaphor of the withered fig tree is "to begin Jesus' ideological project of subverting the temple-centered social order" of Jesus' day.[5]

Mark links Jesus' overturning the tables of the money-changers and the seats of those selling doves. Jesus' subversion of these sales is street theater and protest against the temple's exploitation of the poor; birds were sacrifices for the poor, notably women and lepers. Teaching in the temple the next day, he will speak against such exploitation as he observes a poor widow give her last coin to the temple, a very wealthy institution, to which wealth flowed from all over Judea and Galilee. The money-changers, situated within the temple as in a bank, exchanged Tyrian coins for Roman or Greek money; worshippers and pilgrims would then use these coins for buying sacrifices (animals and other food) and for paying temple taxes and tithes.[6] Herzog writes that to understand Jesus' charge against the temple, we must understand the role that the temple played as a bank in Jerusalem and as a political instrument, dependent on Rome, throughout Judea and Galilee. "Its treasury served as the 'state exchequer' and bank for the aristocracy of Jerusalem." Wealth, derived from monetizing the economy and from loans to the rural poor, flowed into the temple. "At the very apex of this system of exploitation stood the families of the high priests and the lay aristocrats who supported them. . . . The temple was not only a religious and political institution; it was a major economic force, controlling massive amounts of money while continuing to accumulate more. All the functionaries mentioned in the incident in the temple were part of this system and served it."[7]

With "My house will be called a house of prayer for all nations," Jesus cites Isaiah 56:1-8 with an inclusive vision of God and of the temple, the House of the Lord. God insists on justice for all who "maintain justice and do right," including foreigners and outcasts such as eunuchs—although the Torah banned eunuchs from the temple. "By citing prophet against cult in his oracle of judgment against the temple, Jesus has also continued the tradition of God who abrogates and creates anew."[8] God creates anew, and Jesus urges faith and prayer as the way to that new creation. Myers writes, "Faith entails political imagination, the ability to envision a world that is not dominated by the powers."[9] We *can* envision and enable a world of justice, mercy, and love "for all nations."

At a 2009 interfaith prayer action led by Hispanic clergy following the immigration authority's seizure of 361 undocumented women in a New Bedford factory and the death of Mr. Jason Ng in immigration custody, clergy and laity prayed for justice and mercy for

14.1 Interfaith prayer action at statehouse

undocumented immigrants in front of and on the steps of the Rhode Island State House (Illus. 14.1). What do you envision and pray for?

Mark 11:27-33

>[27]Again they came to Jerusalem. As he was walking in the temple, the chief priests, the scribes, and the elders came to him [28]and said, "By what authority are you doing these things? Who gave you this authority to do them?" [29]Jesus said to them, "I will ask you one question; answer me, and I will tell you by what authority I do these things. [30]Did the baptism of John come from heaven, or was it of human origin? Answer me." [31]They argued with one another, "If we say, 'From heaven,' he will say, 'Why then did you not believe him?' [32]But shall we say, 'Of human origin'?"—they were afraid of the crowd, for all regarded John as truly a prophet. [33]So they answered Jesus, "We do not know." And Jesus said to them, "Neither will I tell you by what authority I am doing these things."

14.2 Worship in the spirit of justice

This is the first of three exchanges between the Judean authorities and Jesus over authority. The chief priests, scribes, and the elders signify the authority of the Jerusalem Sanhedrin, the Jewish court in Judea;[10] they have been watching Jesus since his early healing ministry in Galilee, where the scribes challenged Jesus' authority to forgive sins. Jesus refuses to be entrapped by them. Clearly, however, God gave Jesus his authority to heal, to liberate, and to bring justice and mercy to the broken. As David Rhodes writes, "these boundary-crossing events began with Jesus' baptism in the Jordan, when God crossed the boundary between heaven and earth by sending the Holy Spirit to empower Jesus to spread the kingdom."[11]

In Lafayette Square, not far from the White House in Washington, DC, Brian McLaren, then pastor of the Cedar Ridge Church of Columbia, Maryland, claimed that authority and led a "Worship in the Spirit of Justice" with his church on behalf of Darfur, Sudan, in 2005. Word spread of the church's plans, and I traveled with a small group of my church to be part of the worship (Illus. 14.2).

Interfaith political action on behalf of Darfur helped to stop the genocide in the Sudan. We *do* have the authority to act for justice, mercy, and love: to act with the Cedar Ridge Church, the Ginghamsburg United Methodist Church, Martin Luther King, Jr., Dorothy Stang, Jewish Voice for Peace, the "Bread and Blessings" program, Open Table of Christ United Methodist Church, Drs. Raj and Mabel Arole, Archbishop Oscar Romero, the Irish nuns who went to El Salvador, the Coptic and Muslim clerics of Minya—and many, many more, around the world, over generations.

CHAPTER 15

MARK 12 _____

Mark 12:1-12

¹Then he began to speak to them in parables. "A man planted a vineyard, put a fence around it, dug a pit for the wine press, and built a watchtower; then he leased it to tenants and went to another country. ²When the season came, he sent a slave to the tenants to collect from them his share of the produce of the vineyard. ³But they seized him, and beat him, and sent him away empty-handed. ⁴And again he sent another slave to them; this one they beat over the head and insulted. ⁵Then he sent another, and that one they killed. And so it was with many others; some they beat, and others they killed. ⁶He had still one other, a beloved son. Finally he sent him to them, saying, 'They will respect my son.' ⁷But those tenants said to one another, 'This is the heir; come, let us kill him, and the inheritance will be ours.' ⁸So they seized him, killed him, and threw him out of the vineyard. ⁹What then will the owner of the vineyard do? He will come and destroy the tenants and give the vineyard to others. ¹⁰Have you not read this scripture: 'The stone that the builders rejected has become the cornerstone; ¹¹this was the Lord's doing, and it is amazing in our eyes'?" ¹²When they realized that he had told this parable against them, they wanted to arrest him, but they feared the crowd. So they left him and went away.

A traditional interpretation of this challenging parable has been that of an "earthly story with a heavenly meaning."[1] The man who planted the vineyard was God; the rebellious tenant farmers were Israel, and the son was Jesus. Herzog, however, understanding parables as "subversive speech" and Jesus as a pedagogue or teacher of the oppressed, interprets the parable as an "earthy story with heavy meaning" in the context of the Jewish peasant's spiral into debt and loss of land under the burden of first-century taxation and tariffs. In telling such parables, Jesus enabled peasant listeners to analyze their lives and the "systems of oppression that controlled their lives and held them in bondage." In the process, the contradictions between the exploitation and oppression of their daily lives as Jewish peasants and the justice and peace proclaimed for them in their scriptures were obvious.[2] "Because land in Galilee was largely accounted for and intensely cultivated, a 'man' could acquire the land required to build a vineyard only by taking it from someone else. The most likely way he would have added the land to his holdings was through foreclosure on loans to free peasant farmers who were unable to pay off the loans because of poor harvests."[3]

The man was most likely a very wealthy Galilean or Judean member of the elite land-holding class. The tenants most probably were the previous owners, forced into debt; and the listeners to the parable were peasants who would have identified with the tenants and the tragic loss of family land. Herzog proposes that for the listeners, the parable serves both the function of "vicarious thrill of revolt" and the cautionary warning that such revolt would only lead to more tragedy.[4] Concluding the parable with Psalm 118:22-23, the rejected stone becoming the cornerstone of a new creation, Mark presents Jesus as being the alternative to futile violent revolt. Although in coded language, the Jerusalem authorities still know he has told this parable against them.

Mark 12:13-17

[13]Then they sent to him some Pharisees and some Herodians to trap him in what he said. [14]And they came and said to him, "Teacher, we know that you are sincere, and show deference to no one; for you do not regard people with partiality, but teach the way of God in accordance with truth. Is it lawful to pay taxes to the emperor, or not? [15]Should we pay them, or should we not?" But knowing their hypocrisy, he said to them, "Why are you putting me to the test? Bring me a denarius and let me see it." [16]And they brought one. Then he said to them, "Whose head is this, and whose title?" They answered, "The emperor's." [17]Jesus

said to them, "Give to the emperor the things that are the emperor's, and to God the things that are God's." And they were utterly amazed at him.

First, the Jerusalem authorities attempted to entrap Jesus with questions about his authority as he taught in the temple. Jesus followed up with the parable of the rebellious tenants, and now those authorities, who are collaborators with Rome, test his loyalty to Caesar. The Roman Empire required Jews to pay them a poll tax as a sign of subjugation to the empire; it was a very unpopular tax on poor peasants imposed by an army of occupation. To refuse to pay it was to risk being accused of rebellion. To pay it was to be unpopular with the crowds who opposed it. Those who paid it, paid in Roman currency, which Romans insisted upon to unite and monetize the empire. On this coin, a denarius, was an image of the head of Emperor Tiberius as well as inscriptions ascribing divinity to the Caesars. Note that Jesus does not carry such a coin, but these authorities are able to secure one. Jesus' response to give "to God the things that are God's" would have a clear meaning to another Jew: they would have known that the scriptures said that *everything, all of creation*, belonged to God. In this story, as Herzog writes, Jesus' response speaks of "resistance, not accommodation" to Rome.[5]

Mark 12:18-27

[18]Some Sadducees, who say there is no resurrection, came to him and asked him a question, saying, [19]"Teacher, Moses wrote for us that 'if a man's brother dies, leaving a wife but no child, the man shall marry the widow and raise up children for his brother.' [20]There were seven brothers; the first married and, when he died, left no children; [21]and the second married her and died, leaving no children; and the third likewise; [22]none of the seven left children. Last of all the woman herself died. [23]In the resurrection whose wife will she be? For the seven had married her." [24]Jesus said to them, "Is not this the reason you are wrong, that you know neither the scriptures nor the power of God? [25]For when they rise from the dead, they neither marry nor are given in marriage, but are like angels in heaven. [26]And as for the dead

being raised, have you not read in the book of Moses, in the story about the bush, how God said to him, 'I am the God of Abraham, the God of Isaac, and the God of Jacob'? [27]He is God not of the dead, but of the living; you are quite wrong."

Attempts to entrap Jesus continue. The Sadducees, a group of elite, conservative Judeans who don't believe in resurrection, use an extreme instance of levirate marriage, the tradition of a man's being obliged to marry his dead brother's widow if the brother died without leaving any children, to pit the Torah against resurrection. As Myers points out, however, "moral chaos in the resurrection is not the issue; maintenance of socio-economic status through the posterity of the seven sons is."[6] The Sadducees are not concerned about the pain of the woman who did not have children, nor are they concerned that the woman is treated as an object in both life and death. In the Sadducees' challenge, the woman is property. Although the English translation is that of dying "without leaving any children," the Greek is more to the point. The men die without establishing their seed; the woman is merely soil for their seed. The depth of Jesus' disagreement with the classist and patriarchal thinking behind this challenge is revealed in Jesus' response, "You are badly mistaken."

Schüssler Fiorenza interprets this text as a rejection of levirate marriage in the world of the living God. The Sadducees are wrong. "They do not know either the scriptures or the power of God, because they do not recognize that 'in the world' of the living God patriarchal marriage does not exist for men or for women." It's not that sexuality and gender do not exist in the realm of God, but that domination and patriarchal marriage will be no more.[7] God makes all things new.

We trust in the power of God to make all things new—our lives and even our deaths—beyond our imagining. Believe in the possibility of new life, seen in the new life of blind Bartimaeus, the bleeding woman, and the demoniac who lived among the tombs. For followers of Jesus, our brokenness of today is not the end; in faith, in the realm of God, we may experience new life, new hope, and new wholeness. Even death is not the end. Jesus has foretold in three consecutive passion predictions that after three days he will rise. Believing in him, we trust in God's eternal love.

Mark 12:28-34

[28]One of the scribes came near and heard them disputing with one another, and seeing that he answered them well, he asked him, "Which commandment is the first of all?" [29]Jesus answered, "The first is, 'Hear, O Israel: the Lord our God, the Lord is one; [30]you shall love the Lord your God with all your heart, and with all your soul, and with all your mind, and with all your strength.' [31]The second is this, 'You shall love your neighbor as yourself.' There is no other commandment greater than these." [32]Then the scribe said to him, "You are right, Teacher; you have truly said that 'he is one, and besides him there is no other'; [33]and 'to love him with all the heart, and with all the understanding, and with all the strength,' and 'to love one's neighbor as oneself,'—this is much more important than all whole burnt offerings and sacrifices." [34]When Jesus saw that he answered wisely, he said to him, "You are not far from the kingdom of God." After that no one dared to ask him any question.

Jesus has joined together two Hebrew Testament commandments that were not traditionally joined. The first, recited thrice daily by all pious Jews, is Deuteronomy 6:4-9, "Hear, O Israel: the Lord our God, the Lord is one; you shall love the Lord your God with all your heart, and with all your soul, and with all your mind, and with all your strength." The second commandment is a quotation of Leviticus 19:18, "Love your neighbor as yourself." There is little disagreement between Jesus and the scribe, who wisely adds the comment that acting in love is much more important than sacrifice, reflecting the Hebrew scriptures' emphasis on justice and mercy. Myers points out that the commandment to love one's neighbor in Leviticus follows a series of commandments on justice and mercy, each of which concludes "I am the Lord your God" (Lev. 19:9-18). Indeed, it is the "culmination of a litany of commands prohibiting the *oppression and exploitation* of Israel's weak and poor."[8]

> When you reap the harvest of your land, you shall not reap to the very edges of your field, or gather the gleanings of your harvest. You shall not strip your vineyard bare, or gather the fallen grapes

of your vineyard; you shall leave them for the poor and the alien: I am the Lord your God. . . .

You shall not defraud your neighbor; you shall not steal; and you shall not keep for yourself the wages of a laborer until morning. You shall not revile the deaf or put a stumbling-block before the blind; you shall fear your God: I am the Lord.

You shall not render an unjust judgment; you shall not be partial to the poor or defer to the great: with justice you shall judge your neighbor. You shall not go around as a slanderer among your people, and you shall not profit by the blood of your neighbor: I am the Lord.

You shall not hate in your heart anyone of your kin; you shall reprove your neighbor, or you will incur guilt yourself. You shall not take vengeance or bear a grudge against any of your people, but you shall love your neighbor as yourself: I am the Lord.

Love and justice are inseparable, said the great Hebrew prophets. In the eighth century B.C.E., Micah proclaimed (6:6-8), "With what shall I come before the Lord, and bow myself before God on high? Shall I come before him with burnt offerings, with calves a year old? Will the Lord be pleased with thousands of rams, with tens of thousands of rivers of oil? Shall I give my firstborn for my transgression, the fruit of my body for the sin of my soul? He has told you, O mortal, what is good; and what does the Lord require of you but to do justice, and to love kindness, and to walk humbly with your God?" In joining love of God and love of neighbor, Jesus is a faithful Jew rooted in the scriptures.

Who in this interconnected world is our neighbor?

Mark 12:35-37

35While Jesus was teaching in the temple, he said, "How can the scribes say that the Messiah is the son of David? 36David himself, by the Holy Spirit, declared, 'The Lord said to my Lord, "Sit at my right hand, until I put your enemies under your feet."'37David himself calls him Lord; so how can he be his son?" And the large crowd was listening to him with delight.

The debates have ended and Jesus is teaching the crowd, who listen with delight to the man they expect to be the messiah in the tradition of messianic might. Myers writes, "Jesus is not disputing genealogy but ideology: to be 'David's son' is to stand in solidarity" with the imperial tradition of the messiah who restores the temple and Israel as of old. Jesus, however, will not be that messiah.[9] He proceeds to tell them, in the following critique of the scribes and in his compassion for the poor widow why he will not be.

Mark 12:38-44

[38]As he taught, he said, "Beware of the scribes, who like to walk around in long robes, and to be greeted with respect in the marketplaces,[39]and to have the best seats in the synagogues and places of honor at banquets! [40]They devour widows' houses and for the sake of appearance say long prayers. They will receive the greater condemnation." [41]He sat down opposite the treasury, and watched the crowd putting money into the treasury. Many rich people put in large sums. [42]A poor widow came and put in two small copper coins, which are worth a penny. [43]Then he called his disciples and said to them, "Truly I tell you, this poor widow has put in more than all those who are contributing to the treasury. [44]For all of them have contributed out of their abundance; but she out of her poverty has put in everything she had, all she had to live on."

The rich give out of their abundance; the widow gives everything she had to live on. The story of the widow evokes the story of Elijah and the widow who makes a meal for Elijah even though she and her son are starving (1 Kgs. 17:7-24). In response to her faithfulness, God provides food for her and her family every day. Possibly, the story is one of discipleship and faithfulness.

Jesus comments on the widow's giving, however, after he critiqued the scribes' exploitation of widows. Could it be that Jesus' comments convey not admiration for such sacrificial giving, as many of us have been taught in church, but continued critique of temple exploitation? Scribes were trustees of the estates of widows who were not trusted to manage these assets, however meager, simply because they were women. For their efforts, scribes got a percentage of the assets; however, often the system was abused and the widow suffered. As Myers notes, "the vocation of Torah Judaism is to protect 'orphans and widows,' yet in the name of piety these socially vulnerable classes are being exploited while the scribal class is further endowed."[10]

From the beginning of the Gospel of Mark, Jesus has acted and preached to bring wholeness to the most vulnerable. I find it hard to believe, in the context of the dire socio-economic circumstances of first-century Palestine and the status of single women in that society, that Jesus would applaud a widow's giving to the temple her last coin. Starvation and death would follow. Jesus calls for sacrifice to enable justice, mercy, and love—not exploitation for the sake of the institutional church, nor suffering for the sake of suffering.

This barefooted, elderly woman epitomizes such sacrifice for justice in La Paz, Bolivia, in the 1980s. During a time of famine, the stealing of garbage cans by the starving, hyperinflation, and the closing of tin mines leading to the unemployment of thousands, women took to the streets to peacefully demonstrate for justice. Marching through the

15.1 Bolivian woman returning from a protest

streets singing, chanting, and banging their cooking pots together in a great clatter, they protested the international monetary actions that brought further hunger and misery into their homes. Catholic and Protestant clergy walked at their sides. This woman was returning home from one of those demonstrations and was about to climb the path to her one-room adobe house in the hard-scrabble hills above the road, near my home (Illus. 15.1).

Justice has not yet come to the poor of Bolivia. The church, however, in many instances stands with the poor, as they continue to peacefully march and demonstrate for justice; the Evangelical Methodist Church is one that has been active for decades. In a 2005 pastoral letter, the Methodist bishop wrote,

> We are asking all members of the Evangelical Methodist Church in Bolivia to not give up as we face these times of adversity, to hear God's word with renewed faith and hope, to be vigilant and in constant prayer on behalf of our country, for our communities and for our church, to intercede and accompany our Methodist brothers who participate in mobilizations and marches from the rural area, in a spirit and acts of solidarity, from our pastoral and prophetic mission perspective.[11]

As Jesus will say in the next text, this is "the beginning of the birth-pangs . . . but the one who endures to the end will be saved."

CHAPTER 16

MARK 13 ⎯⎯⎯⎯⎯⎯⎯⎯⎯⎯⎯⎯⎯⎯

Mark 13:1-37

¹As he came out of the temple, one of his disciples said to him, "Look, Teacher, what large stones and what large buildings!" ²Then Jesus asked him, "Do you see these great buildings? Not one stone will be left here upon another; all will be thrown down." ³When he was sitting on the Mount of Olives opposite the temple, Peter, James, John, and Andrew asked him privately, ⁴"Tell us, when will this be, and what will be the sign that all these things are about to be accomplished?" ⁵Then Jesus began to say to them, "Beware that no one leads you astray. ⁶Many will come in my name and say, 'I am he!' and they will lead many astray. ⁷When you hear of wars and rumors of wars, do not be alarmed; this must take place, but the end is still to come. ⁸For nation will rise against nation, and kingdom against kingdom; there will be earthquakes in various places; there will be famines. This is but the beginning of the birthpangs. ⁹"As for yourselves, beware; for they will hand you over to councils; and you will be beaten in synagogues; and you will stand before governors and kings because of me, as a testimony to them. ¹⁰And the good news must first be proclaimed to all nations. ¹¹When they bring you to trial and hand you over, do not worry beforehand about what you are to say; but say whatever is given you at that time, for it is not you who speak, but the Holy Spirit. ¹²Brother will betray brother to death, and a father his child, and children will rise against parents and have them put to death; ¹³and you will be hated by all because of my name. But the one who endures to the end will be saved.

¹⁴"But when you see the desolating sacrilege set up where it ought not to be (let the reader understand), then those in Judea

must flee to the mountains; [15]the one on the housetop must not go down or enter the house to take anything away; [16]the one in the field must not turn back to get a coat. [17]Woe to those who are pregnant and to those who are nursing infants in those days! [18]Pray that it may not be in winter. [19]For in those days there will be suffering, such as has not been from the beginning of the creation that God created until now, no, and never will be. [20]And if the Lord had not cut short those days, no one would be saved; but for the sake of the elect, whom he chose, he has cut short those days. [21]And if anyone says to you at that time, 'Look! Here is the Messiah!' or 'Look! There he is!'—do not believe it. [22]False messiahs and false prophets will appear and produce signs and omens, to lead astray, if possible, the elect. [23]But be alert; I have already told you everything.

[24]"But in those days, after that suffering, the sun will be darkened, and the moon will not give its light, [25]and the stars will be falling from heaven, and the powers in the heavens will be shaken. [26]Then they will see 'the Son of Man coming in clouds' with great power and glory. [27]Then he will send out the angels, and gather his elect from the four winds, from the ends of the earth to the ends of heaven.

[28]"From the fig tree learn its lesson: as soon as its branch becomes tender and puts forth its leaves, you know that summer is near. [29]So also, when you see these things taking place, you know that he is near, at the very gates. [30]Truly I tell you, this generation will not pass away until all these things have taken place. [31]Heaven and earth will pass away, but my words will not pass away.

[32]"But about that day or hour no one knows, neither the angels in heaven, nor the Son, but only the Father. [33]Beware, keep alert; for you do not know when the time will come. [34]It is like a man going on a journey, when he leaves home and puts his slaves in charge, each with his work, and commands the doorkeeper to be on the watch. [35]Therefore, keep awake—for you do not know when the master of the house will come, in the evening, or at midnight, or at cockcrow, or at dawn, [36]or else he may find you asleep when he comes suddenly. [37]And what I say to you I say to all: Keep awake."

Mark 13 is apocalyptic literature, which is to say, it is revelatory literature. It is a way of seeing through the oppression and suffering of present life to the ultimate reality and justice of God. Apocalyptic literature presents the reality of evil—together with the reassurance that our God is a God of justice. Whoever endures in faith, in nonviolent resistance to evil, will see that God is with them. In the end, there will be justice. Myers writes that the heart of Mark's apocalyptic argument is that Jesus' death (the crucifixion of the Son of Man, or the Human One) and "his revelation 'in power and glory' are the same moment. It is through his demonstration of the nonviolent power of the cross that the powers are overthrown."[1]

Apocalyptic imagery, as literature of the oppressed, has great meaning for many black Americans and our immigrant sisters and brothers, who recall terrible suffering and terror. In a recent Bible study of Mark, when we came to this text, a normally quiet Liberian immigrant friend began to tremble and then burst out with memories of fleeing and hiding during the Liberian civil war. With a baby on her back and hungry terrified children in hand, she ran and hid in the bush, fell, picked herself up, carried the children, and hid again for days from crazed troops, rape, mutilation, and death. When Brian McLaren and his community stood one block from the White House praying for an end to the genocide in the Sudan, they were standing in witness against such terror. Others stood, in terror, before Latin American councils and civil authorities testifying for their lives and the lives of others, praying for justice. Others like Dorothy Stang and Martin Luther King, Jr., died in their commitment to "stay awake" until the end.

With allusions to Jewish apocalyptic text that would have been familiar to Mark's listeners, Mark probably wrote this "Little Apocalypse"[2] during the Judean revolt of 66–70 C.E. Myers writes that the critical question for Mark's community at that time was whether, as followers of Jesus, they should join forces with the rebels against Rome. In Mark's text, Jesus speaks to this community, warning against the temptation to use violence to combat violence. For several years, parts of Palestine were liberated; there was a provisional government. "Rebel recruiters were going throughout Palestine summoning Jews to Jerusalem's defense." Myers suggests that "Mark's community was critical of both imperial collaborators and nationalists. Its nonviolent stance, refusing to cooperate with either the Jewish guerrillas or the Roman counterinsurgency, earned it persecution from both sides of the war."[3] Mary Ann Tolbert, writing from a similar perspective, describes this text as "resistance literature."[4]

Jesus' prediction of the fall of the temple, one of the architectural wonders of the ancient world, will be one of the charges brought against him by the Sanhedrin. If, after his royal entry into Jerusalem, he did make such a prediction in the tradition of the Hebrew prophets, the Jewish and Roman authorities would have been very alarmed. The temple, in addition to being the center of Jewish worship, was the center for Roman occupation and the Jewish financial center. Josephus described it, "Even the outward face of the temple in its front wanted nothing that was likely to surprise either men's minds or their eyes: for it was covered all over with plates of gold of great weight, and at the first rising of the sun, reflected back a very fiery splendor, and made those who forced themselves to look upon it to turn their eyes away, just as they would have done with the sun's own rays."[5] Herzog writes, "The destruction of the oppressive institution that the temple had become was one step toward the coming justice of the reign of God, who gathers the outcasts and foreigners and invites them to build a community, where in the words of Isaiah 'in righteousness you shall be established; you shall be far from oppression; for you shall not fear; and from terror, for it shall not come near you. Maintain justice, and do what is right; for soon my salvation will come and my deliverance shall be revealed.' The symbolic destruction of the temple was a prelude to the coming justice of a different kind of reign, the reign of God."[6]

Mark's generation will see the end of the temple-state, but Jesus' words will not pass away. This is the lesson of the fig tree. Rome began the final siege and assault on Jerusalem in the spring of 70 C.E. People who had fled into Jerusalem for safety died horribly. Josephus wrote that over a million people died of starvation and the sword, and 97,000 people were taken captive. The tallest and handsomest youth were kept for the triumphal processional in Rome, "of the rest, those over seventeen were put in irons and sent to the mines in Egypt or presented to the provinces to be destroyed by sword or beast in the theaters. Those under seventeen were sold."[7] The Romans burned the temple and the great stones tumbled to the ground.

Mark asserts that God is faithful and God is just. In this world of genocide in Africa, war in the Middle East, bread lines in our own cities and towns, foreclosed homes, and an increasing divide between the poor and wealthy of the world, what does it mean for us to be faithful? What does it mean today to stay awake and watch?

CHAPTER 17

MARK 14

Mark 14:1-11

[1]It was two days before the Passover and the festival of Unleavened Bread. The chief priests and the scribes were looking for a way to arrest Jesus by stealth and kill him; [2]for they said, "Not during the festival, or there may be a riot among the people." [3]While he was at Bethany in the house of Simon the leper, as he sat at the table, a woman came with an alabaster jar of very costly ointment of nard, and she broke open the jar and poured the ointment on his head. [4]But some were there who said to one another in anger, "Why was the ointment wasted in this way? [5]For this ointment could have been sold for more than three hundred denarii, and the money given to the poor." And they scolded her. [6]But Jesus said, "Let her alone; why do you trouble her? She has performed a good service for me. [7]For you always have the poor with you, and you can show kindness to them whenever you wish; but you will not always have me. [8]She has done what she could; she has anointed my body beforehand for its burial. [9]Truly I tell you, wherever the good news is proclaimed in the whole world, what she has done will be told in remembrance of her." [10]Then Judas Iscariot, who was one of the twelve, went to the chief priests in order to betray him to them. [11]When they heard it, they were greatly pleased, and promised to give him money. So he began to look for an opportunity to betray him.

Passover, the great story of God's liberation of the Jews from slavery in Egypt, brought Jews throughout the empire to Jerusalem. Liberation was in the festival air. As Moses had led their ancestors out of slavery, so might a messiah in their times bring liberation to them. Reclining in the home of a leper, that messiah, Jesus, is about two miles outside the city, at the foot of the Mount of Olives. He will bring liberation, but not as the Judean authorities, the crowds, or even his disciples expect. In his nonviolent walk to the cross, Jesus will show his believers a new way to new life.

At a meal with his friends as the tension rises, again a woman bursts upon the scene in defiance of societal norms. Outside of Tyre, a nameless Syrophoenecian woman wanted healing for her daughter and in the process opened Jesus' ministry to the Gentiles. Now, outside of Jerusalem, another nameless woman reaches beyond those norms and in the process anoints Jesus as the king who is about to die. In the Hebrew Testament, kings were anointed with the pouring of perfume upon their heads. In Jewish tradition, the dead were anointed with spices and perfumes for burial; this nameless woman is a prophet, recognizing that Jesus, her king, is about to die. She is the first of his followers fully to grasp the nature of Jesus. Schüssler Fiorenza identifies the woman's action as "a prophetic sign action," an anointing of Jesus as "the messianic inaugurator of the *basileia* (the kingdom)."[1]

Jesus' statement, "For you always have the poor with you, and you can show kindness to them whenever you wish," is easily misunderstood. Jesus is paraphrasing two lines from Deuteronomy, "There will always be poor people in the land. Therefore I command you to be openhanded toward those of your people who are poor and needy in the land" (15:11). They are within a series of directives to reduce poverty and promote justice that seventh-century B.C.E. scriptural writers described as commandments of God to Moses. In citing them, Mark assumes hearers understand the context: God's commandments to do justice. Rather than Jesus' callous acceptance of poverty, which would be totally out of character, Jesus is saying that his followers will always be among the poor and showing kindness to the poor. Jesus will not be with them for long; now he is being prepared for his death and burial.

In this story of the woman's "prophetic sign action," Schüssler Fiorenza sees Jesus demonstrating a solidarity with women that his followers failed to uphold after the early years of the movement, as they also failed to uphold solidarity with the poor. She writes, "The 'church of the poor' and the 'church of women' must be recovered at the same time, if 'solidarity from below' is to become a reality for the whole community of Jesus again. As a feminist vision, the basileia vision of

Jesus calls all women without exception to wholeness and selfhood, as well as to solidarity with those women who are the impoverished, the maimed, and the outcasts of our society and church."[2] It is for believers a new way to new life. Judas Iscariot will not be one of them. Mark does not tell us why he betrays Jesus. His betrayal only stands in sharp contrast to the nameless woman's faithfulness. How ironic that Mark says the story will be told in memory of her—but he neglects to tell the reader her name!

Mark 14:12-25

[12]On the first day of Unleavened Bread, when the Passover lamb is sacrificed, his disciples said to him, "Where do you want us to go and make the preparations for you to eat the Passover?" [13]So he sent two of his disciples, saying to them, "Go into the city, and a man carrying a jar of water will meet you; follow him, [14]and wherever he enters, say to the owner of the house, 'The Teacher asks, Where is my guest room where I may eat the Passover with my disciples?' [15]He will show you a large room upstairs, furnished and ready. Make preparations for us there." [16]So the disciples set out and went to the city, and found everything as he had told them; and they prepared the Passover meal. [17]When it was evening, he came with the twelve. [18]And when they had taken their places and were eating, Jesus said, "Truly I tell you, one of you will betray me, one who is eating with me." [19]They began to be distressed and to say to him one after another, "Surely, not I?" [20]He said to them, "It is one of the twelve, one who is dipping bread into the bowl with me. [21]For the Son of Man goes as it is written of him, but woe to that one by whom the Son of Man is betrayed! It would have been better for that one not to have been born." [22]While they were eating, he took a loaf of bread, and after blessing it he broke it, gave it to them, and said, "Take; this is my body." [23]Then he took a cup, and after giving thanks he gave it to them, and all of them drank from it. [24]He said to them, "This is my blood of the covenant, which is poured out for many. [25]Truly I tell you, I will never again drink of the fruit of the vine until that day when I drink it new in the kingdom of God."

In preparation for the Passover, the disciples are a larger group than the twelve; Jesus sends two ahead to prepare the meal and twelve arrive later with him. Despite the crowds, the man carrying a water jug, normally women's work, is identified. He must have been an additional "disciple," which comes from the Indo-European root *dek*, which means "to accept, to take," or "to learn." In this Last Supper, Jesus takes, blesses, breaks, and gives his body and his blood; the disciples take and learn. We, as those who also take and learn, are disciples as well.

Jesus took a loaf of bread, broken to represent his impending broken body, one loaf broken into pieces sufficient to feed his many disciples in the room. One loaf was enough that night even as five loaves were enough to feed five thousand people by the lake days before. We do not take the bread and wine alone; we are part of a new covenant and a new community formed out of Jesus' life and death, across all time and space. When we share the wine, "the blood of the new covenant," we share in an agreement between God and God's people. We hear the promises of God and the requirements and the call upon us in return. When Jesus speaks of that covenant, he invokes the stories of his people who heard God's call and set out in response. Abraham and Sarah left their homeland and ancestored a new community. Israel became a people in relationship with God during the Exodus from Egypt. In our own times, we share the bread and wine in solidarity with all who hunger.

One who shared in solidarity was Archbishop Oscar Romero of El Salvador, assassinated in 1980 by a government killer as he held mass in a hospital chapel, near the new National Cathedral in the nation's capital. A few years before his assassination, Romero had been a conservative bishop welcomed by that same right-wing Salvadoran government.[3] Shortly after his appointment as archbishop, however, the murder of a Jesuit friend working with peasants for land reform opened his eyes to his country's injustice and oppression. The cathedral became the center of his advocacy for justice, pleas for peace, and critique of the government. As a symbol of the church's solidarity with the poor, Romero insisted that the in-process decoration of the new cathedral remain unfinished as long as there were poor and hungry people in the country. When I was there in 2000, the decoration remained unfinished, with exposed metal rafters in the ceiling, plastic chairs for the congregation, and empty niches behind the altar for sacred art. That space lives in my memory as a challenge to be more faithful, as does Oscar Romero, who learned and then taught the meaning of taking, blessing, breaking, and giving his body and his blood.

Mark 14:26-31

26When they had sung the hymn, they went out to the Mount of Olives. 27And Jesus said to them, "You will all become deserters; for it is written, 'I will strike the shepherd, and the sheep will be scattered.' 28But after I am raised up, I will go before you to Galilee." 29Peter said to him, "Even though all become deserters, I will not." 30Jesus said to him, "Truly I tell you, this day, this very night, before the cock crows twice, you will deny me three times." 31But he said vehemently, "Even though I must die with you, I will not deny you." And all of them said the same.

Again Jesus quotes the Hebrew scriptures. The metaphor of the shepherd and the sheep is from Zechariah 13, where God strikes down an unfaithful shepherd. Jesus, however, is a faithful shepherd, so Mark's text may reflect the early church's bewildered trust in God; they don't understand why their good shepherd should have been crucified. At the same time, Jesus promises the ultimate vindication of goodness. He will be raised up and go before his disciples to Galilee.

Mark 14:32-42

32They went to a place called Gethsemane; and he said to his disciples, "Sit here while I pray." 33He took with him Peter and James and John, and began to be distressed and agitated. 34And he said to them, "I am deeply grieved, even to death; remain here, and keep awake." 35And going a little farther, he threw himself on the ground and prayed that, if it were possible, the hour might pass from him. 36He said, "Abba, Father, for you all things are possible; remove this cup from me; yet, not what I want, but what you want." 37He came and found them sleeping; and he said to Peter, "Simon, are you asleep? Could you not keep awake one hour? 38Keep awake and pray that you may not come into the time of trial; the spirit indeed is willing, but the flesh is weak." [39]And again he went away and prayed, saying the same words. [40]And once more he came and found them sleeping, for their eyes were very heavy; and they did not know what to say to him. [41]He came a third time and said to them, "Are you still sleeping and taking your rest? Enough! The hour has come; the Son of Man is betrayed into the hands of sinners. [42]Get up, let us be going. See, my betrayer is at hand."

Jesus prays at Gethsemane, which means "olive press" in Hebrew. Here on the Mount of Olives, where olives were squashed and pressed into liquid, Jesus, the Human One, who brought wholeness to others, is agitated and grieving. Knowing that sooner or later the authorities would seize him and he would die a tortured death, he seeks the comfort of his friends, but they fail him. He voices the laments of the Psalms, particularly Psalms 42 and 43, three times crying out to God, confessing his faith in God, and imploring God for God's help. In the sorrowful recounting of Gethsemane, Mark includes language found in the Lord's Prayer of the later Gospels. "Jesus addresses God as 'Abba, Father . . . He prays that God's will may be done . . . and he asks that his disciples not 'enter into testing.'"[4]

The pathos of Gethsemane is overwhelming. Jesus is alone and broken. How could the disciples fall asleep on him? In the "Little Apocalypse" of 13:35-37, he predicted terrible days ahead and warned the disciples to stay awake; now, they are at least metaphorically asleep. They still don't understand that Jesus is going to his death. They don't understand the meaning of his life and imminent death or the meaning of their call as disciples. In a world of great injustice, it is all too easy to close one's eyes to that injustice and metaphorically to go to sleep. The disciples of today, identified in this book, have stayed awake.

I think of a group of Irish nuns I met at the Maryknoll Latin American Mission Center in Cochabamba, Bolivia, two years after Archbishop Romero was murdered at the altar. We were all studying Spanish at the Maryknoll Language Institute in preparation for work in Latin America, I in Bolivia, and they in El Salvador. Young, fun-loving, and faithful, they had recently arrived from Ireland and were on their way to replace nuns slain by the Salvadoran military some months before the archbishop's own murder. By raping, torturing, and killing Maryknoll sisters Maura Clarke and Ita Ford, Ursuline sister Dorothy Kazel, and lay missioner Jean Donovan, who were ministering with war refugees at Romero's instruction, the right-wing government meant to intimidate the archbishop and his movement for justice and peace.

It did not intimidate the movement. I don't know what happened to my friends; we did not keep in touch. I do know that the persecution and murder of Catholic leaders committed to reform and justice in El Salvador did not cease until finally the United States, the ally of the rightist Salvadoran government, and the international community intervened after the Salvadoran military murdered six Jesuit scholars and priests and their housekeeper and her daughter at the University of Central America in San Salvador in 1989. In time, a negotiated peace and a partial accounting of the government's role in these murders were reached. The archbishop, the Jesuit scholars, the nuns, and the laity with them still stand as disciples who stayed awake.

Mark 14:43-52

[43]Immediately, while he was still speaking, Judas, one of the twelve, arrived; and with him there was a crowd with swords and clubs, from the chief priests, the scribes, and the elders. [44]Now the betrayer had given them a sign, saying, "The one I will kiss is the man; arrest him and lead him away under guard." [45]So when he came, he went up to him at once and said, "Rabbi!" and kissed him. [46]Then they laid hands on him and arrested him. [47]But one of those who stood near drew his sword and struck the slave of the high priest, cutting off his ear. [48]Then Jesus said to them, "Have you come out with swords and clubs to arrest me as though I were a bandit? [49]Day after day I was with you in the temple teaching, and you did not arrest me. But let the scriptures be fulfilled." [50]All of them deserted him and fled. [51]A certain young man was following him, wearing nothing but a linen cloth. They caught hold of him, [52]but he left the linen cloth and ran off naked.

Crowds followed and acclaimed Jesus throughout his ministry; the Judean authorities had feared those crowds and hesitated to seize Jesus while he was among them. Now in the darkness this crowd, led by the betrayer Judas and recruited by the Judean authorities, carry swords and clubs to seize him, as if he were a bandit or violent revolutionary. Some scholars speculate that there were three groups at Gethsemane that night: the disciples, the crowd, and bystanders who, alarmed by the noise in the night, came to see what was going on.[5] Two nameless people in this scene of betrayal and desertion may have been such bystanders—the person who cuts off the ear of the high priest's servant and the young man who flees naked.

New Testament scholar Raymond Brown thinks that, for Mark, it is most likely that the sword-wielder and the young man who fled naked were bystanders drawn from their beds by the noise and immediately attracted to Jesus, as were the earlier disciples. The sword wielder would not have understood Jesus' nonviolent mission, and he intervened impetuously, out of ignorance. The young man who tried to follow Jesus might have been the "last person to be attracted to the following of Jesus even when all the others have fled. This would-be follower becomes 'the last disciple.'"[6] In his nakedness, he represents the disciples' shame as they all fled in fear, leaving Jesus alone with the murderous crowd. Gerd Theissen speculates that these two, identified as supporters of Jesus in Gethsemane, were unnamed to protect them from Roman retaliation as the oral stories of Jesus circulated in the early years of the movement.[7]

What a long way we have come from the swords and clubs of the Roman Empire. They seem almost innocent compared to Hitler's murderous ovens, our nuclear bombs, and our robotic drones. Although Jesus disavowed violence even to protect himself and his mission, few Christians in the two thousand years since his crucifixion have stood resolutely against violence as he did. In the 2002 Congressional vote on a preemptive American attack on Iraq, only a minority stood against the imperial war on the oil-rich country alleged to have weapons of mass destruction. History proved it did not have nuclear weapons, nor had it reconstituted its chemical and biological weapons. But the American decision to follow in the footsteps of the Roman soldiers in Gethsemane led to global tragedy. The financial cost is estimated to be "$800 billion and climbing."[8] By September 11, 2011, almost 4,500 American military men and women had been killed and over 33,000 wounded, many grievously maimed.[9] The toll on Iraq was much greater. There have been an estimated 102,000 to 112,000 civilian deaths, double that number of casualties and 1.5 million "internally displaced people" living in UN refugee camps. Two epidemiologists in 2006, treating "the war as a public health catastrophe" estimated a "probable 'excess mortality'" of over 600,000 Iraqis who had died since the onset of the war, "but who would not be dead were it not for the war."[10]

Modern warfare is hell for all those intimately involved; it can be absolutely lifelong hell for those badly wounded in poor countries, such as Iraq and Afghanistan. One Ramadan, the Muslim holy month, in Dhaka, Bangladesh, I had a glimpse of some of the effects of modern warfare on the poor, long after the guns had stopped. Bangladesh was a desperately poor country that had fought a brutal civil war to achieve its independence some twenty years previous. In the months leading up to Ramadan, beggars had stood at most street corners in the densely congested city. As vehicles or rickshaws stalled in the heavy traffic or at traffic lights, they, adults and children, the blind, the maimed and the elderly, moved with outstretched hands, asking for a few coins. During Ramadan, however, the expectation of charity was greater, and families brought out the most severely disabled. One day, I rode on a wide road lined with elegant homes behind tall walls near the American Embassy. As my car drove slowly over the speed bumps, on the sidewalk a poorly dressed man and woman stood beside a handmade wheelbarrow. As the car slowed for the speed bump by which they stood, they reached into the wheelbarrow, lifted out a log-like object and rolled it into the street before us, forcing the car to a sudden, complete stop. It was a living human being, a casualty of the war. The begging couple reached into the window, received a few coins, picked up the person on the street, and returned him or her to the wheelbarrow.

How many handmade wheelbarrows with such casualties are there in Iraq and Afghanistan? In the face of such brokenness, the Human One calls to us. As Sharon Thornton reminds us, Jesus "did not give up the way of justice even when injustice was done to him. He lived the power of love and justice by not succumbing to injustice to break the cycle of violence perpetuated by an 'eye for an eye' way of life. Furthermore, he claimed this possibility for others as well. Jesus claimed the vulnerability of a human being whose power lay in the truth of right relationships."[11] Justice and love are inseparable in the realm of God.

Mark 14:53-72

[53]They took Jesus to the high priest; and all the chief priests, the elders, and the scribes were assembled. [54]Peter had followed him at a distance, right into the courtyard of the high priest; and he was sitting with the guards, warming himself at the fire. [55]Now the chief priests and the whole council were looking for testimony against Jesus to put him to death; but they found none. [56]For many gave false testimony against him, and their testimony did not agree. [57]Some stood up and gave false testimony against him, saying, [58]"We heard him say, 'I will destroy this temple that is made with hands, and in three days I will build another, not made with hands.'" [59]But even on this point their testimony did not agree. [60]Then the high priest stood up before them and asked Jesus, "Have you no answer? What is it that they testify against you?" [61]But he was silent and did not answer. Again the high priest asked him, "Are you the Messiah, the Son of the Blessed One?" [62]Jesus said, "I am; and 'you will see the Son of Man seated at the right hand of the Power, and coming with the clouds of heaven.'" [63]Then the high priest tore his clothes and said, "Why do we still need witnesses? [64]You have heard his blasphemy! What is your decision?" All of them condemned him as deserving death. [65]Some began to spit on him, to blindfold him, and to strike him, saying to him, "Prophesy!" The guards also took him over and beat him. [66]While Peter was below in the courtyard, one of the servant-girls of the high priest came by. [67]When she saw Peter warming himself, she stared at him and said, "You also were with Jesus, the man from Nazareth." [68]But he denied it, saying, "I do not know or understand what you are talking about." And he went out into the forecourt. Then the cock crowed. [69]And the servant-girl, on seeing him, began again to say to the bystanders, "This man is one of them." [70]But again he denied it. Then after a little while the bystanders again said to Peter, "Certainly you are one of them; for you are a Galilean." [71]But he began to curse,

and he swore an oath, "I do not know this man you are talking about." [72]At that moment the cock crowed for the second time. Then Peter remembered that Jesus had said to him, "Before the cock crows twice, you will deny me three times." And he broke down and wept.

The recruited crowd of darkness takes Jesus to the home of the chief priest, which, according to Josephus, was an old palace opposite the temple. There on the second floor the Judean authorities await him, away from the crowds that had followed and who would protect him. Below in the courtyard is Peter, wanting to be faithful, wanting to be courageous, yet so scared, like many of us when terrible choices confront us. Would we have been more courageous than he?

The charges against Jesus are twofold: threats to destroy the temple and blasphemy. Mark makes it clear that in this mock trial the Judean authorities consider him guilty and are just looking for evidence to prove it. The authorities have sought to kill him since early in his ministry. Now they have him in a nighttime trial with inconsistent testimony and false witnesses, a trial irregular under Jewish law, in a nation under foreign occupation. Herzog writes, "The Jerusalem elites had reasons enough to collaborate with their Roman overlords to execute the troublesome prophet from Galilee. It was in their political self-interest. . . . They were not acting as 'Jews' nor were their actions particularly 'Jewish.' Their actions and reactions were mostly determined by their social location and ruling class values. They were first-century Judean rulers and retainers with a great deal at stake in maintaining internal order to please their colonial masters."[12]

Jesus refuses to play along with the mockery of a show trial and is silent before the testimony about the temple. After a ministry in which he avoided discussion about being the messiah lest the people misunderstand what type of messiah he would be, Jesus affirms that he is the messiah, the son of the Blessed One, or God. Alone, deserted, powerless and knowing that he is going to his death, Jesus acknowledges this calling and declares his vindication and triumph as the Human One (Son of Man) "at the right hand of the Power," a way of referring to God in Jewish writing that refers to "God working in the world."[13] Although Jesus is powerless at this moment, he is the son of a God working in the world for justice, mercy, and love. Evoking the visions of the prophet Daniel with the allusion "Coming with the clouds of heaven," the dominion and glory of Jesus' God are proclaimed and the temporary power of Caesar is negated. Justice will prevail.

The Jewish punishment for blasphemy was stoning. Jesus, however, was not stoned but turned over to the Romans, perhaps because Roman authorities had to approve capital punishment and probably because the Roman authorities also wanted him. First, he is mocked, abused, and beaten. He is all alone.

For two thousand years, Jesus' faith and integrity have stood in contrast to Peter's cowardice and denial of Jesus. At this point in Mark's story, we could exclaim of Peter, "What a disciple!" Safe in the religious freedom of the United States, it may be hard to identify with Peter's fear and denial. In other parts of the world where hostility to Christianity and discrimination against Christians are intense and deadly—northern Nigeria, Mali, and parts of the Middle East—however, his fear is understandable.

Peter became a new man after the crucifixion, and the rock upon which the church was built. The good news is that people of faith do

17.1 Coptic and Muslim clergy in Minya

gain the courage to work for the peaceful transformation of the world, despite the odds, and they are doing so around the world, every day, in unpublicized ways. In 2004 I was impressed by the courage this Coptic Orthodox priest and Muslim cleric expressed by working together across religious hostilities in rural Minya, Egypt (Illus. 17.1). Defying culture and presenting a united front on the practice of female genital cutting, they jointly gave health education talks from their faith perspectives to eliminate the ancient practice, an African tradition perpetuated for millennia in Egypt by a vast majority of Christians and Muslims alike. In the years since I took this photo, Muslim-Christian conflict in Minya has intensified. Dozens of Christians have died, churches have been burnt, and homes destroyed. The efforts of these two men and the efforts of many others have not been in vain, however; the prevalence of female genital cutting has declined in Egypt.

CHAPTER 18

MARK 15

Mark 15:1-15

¹As soon as it was morning, the chief priests held a consultation with the elders and scribes and the whole council. They bound Jesus, led him away, and handed him over to Pilate. ²Pilate asked him, "Are you the King of the Jews?" He answered him, "You say so." ³Then the chief priests accused him of many things. ⁴Pilate asked him again, "Have you no answer? See how many charges they bring against you." ⁵But Jesus made no further reply, so that Pilate was amazed. ⁶Now at the festival he used to release a prisoner for them, anyone for whom they asked. ⁷Now a man called Barabbas was in prison with the rebels who had committed murder during the insurrection. ⁸So the crowd came and began to ask Pilate to do for them according to his custom. ⁹Then he answered them, "Do you want me to release for you the King of the Jews?" ¹⁰For he realized that it was out of jealousy that the chief priests had handed him over. ¹¹But the chief priests stirred up the crowd to have him release Barabbas for them instead. ¹²Pilate spoke to them again, "Then what do you wish me to do with the man you call the King of the Jews?" ¹³They shouted back, "Crucify him!" ¹⁴Pilate asked them, "Why, what evil has he done?" But they shouted all the more, "Crucify him!" ¹⁵So Pilate, wishing to satisfy the crowd, released Barabbas for them; and after flogging Jesus, he handed him over to be crucified.

The Sanhedrin and the accusers at the Roman trial are similar in a number of ways. The Sanhedrin accuse Jesus of identifying himself as the messiah; the Romans accuse him of being King of the Jews, a charge equivalent to rebellion. Additionally in each trial, as Myers notes, there

are "trumped-up charges that are ironically fitting, two-fold interrogation, a presiding judge [who] consults with others and then convicts,
and final ridicule and torture . . . Judean and Roman authorities are
fully cooperative in their railroading Jesus whom they perceive as a
common enemy."[1] Jesus maintains his integrity and dignity, continuing in his refusal to play along with the charades of these trials. Mark
portrays him as the Suffering Servant of Isaiah 53:7-8:

> He was oppressed, and he was afflicted, yet he did not open his
> mouth; like a lamb that is led to the slaughter, and like a sheep
> that before its shearers is silent, so he did not open his mouth.
> By a perversion of justice he was taken away. Who could have
> imagined his future?

Mark presents Pilate as a weak man who believes Jesus to be innocent, but who defers to the manipulation of the Judean authorities and
the cries of the Jewish crowd for crucifixion.[2] First-century accounts
of Pilate, however, describe him as a vicious and cruel man who would
have had no concern for the innocence of a humble Jewish man. Pilate
was expedient and self-advancing, above all. It is Pilate himself who has
Jesus flogged.

A sadistic prelude to torturous crucifixion, flogging was carried
out with leather whips studded with bone, lead, or hooks that tore
the flesh off the condemned's bones; lengthy flogging would hasten a
man's death on the cross. Only Rome had the authority to crucify, the
Roman penalty for insurrection, meant to terrify onlookers. Crosses
were erected on principal roads and hilltops so the suffering of an
immobilized man, subject to the attacks of vultures, insects, and scav-
enger dogs, would be seen as widely as possible. Some scholars doubt
that a Jewish crowd would implore a Roman ruler to crucify another
Jew.[3] Mark indicates, however, that this manipulated crowd—most
certainly not the same crowd that followed him into Jerusalem—not
only "chooses" freedom for the known murderer over a known healer,
but they also shouted out repeatedly for the healer's crucifixion.[4]
Barabbas, the rebel or bandit of known violence in a recent insurrection, will go free, while the man of known nonviolence will die a
violent death reserved for rebels and revolutionaries.

Mark 15:16-32

¹⁶Then the soldiers led him into the courtyard of the palace (that is, the governor's headquarters); and they called together the whole cohort. ¹⁷And they clothed him in a purple cloak; and after twisting some thorns into a crown, they put it on him. ¹⁸And they began saluting him, "Hail, King of the Jews!" ¹⁹They struck his head with a reed, spat upon him, and knelt down in homage to him. ²⁰After mocking him, they stripped him of the purple cloak and put his own clothes on him. Then they led him out to crucify him. ²¹They compelled a passer-by, who was coming in from the country, to carry his cross; it was Simon of Cyrene, the father of Alexander and Rufus. ²²Then they brought Jesus to the place called Golgotha (which means the place of a skull). ²³And they offered him wine mixed with myrrh; but he did not take it. ²⁴And they crucified him, and divided his clothes among them, casting lots to decide what each should take. ²⁵It was nine o'clock in the morning when they crucified him. ²⁶The inscription of the charge against him read, "The King of the Jews." ²⁷And with him they crucified two bandits, one on his right and one on his left. ²⁹Those who passed by derided him, shaking their heads and saying, "Aha! You who would destroy the temple and build it in three days, ³⁰save yourself, and come down from the cross!" ³¹In the same way the chief priests, along with the scribes, were also mocking him among themselves and saying, "He saved others; he cannot save himself. ³²Let the Messiah, the King of Israel, come down from the cross now, so that we may see and believe." Those who were crucified with him also taunted him.

The Roman soldiers, by calling out the whole cohort of soldiers to watch Jesus' flogging and crucifixion, treat Jesus as a serious threat to Rome: a cohort consisted of about six hundred men. Among this crowd of soldiers, Jesus is alone and beaten: they torture, mock, and humiliate him still further as the King of the Jews. The Roman message is clear: Rome is supreme; there can be no other king and no other son of God than Caesar. Usually, the condemned carried his cross beam to the site of crucifixion, where he was either nailed or tied to it before it was hoisted into place onto the upright beam. Jesus must have been too weakened from torture to carry it; hence Simon, the passer-by from the ancient Greco-Roman city of Cyrene, now in modern Libya, was pressed into action. Simon may have been a Jew arriving in the city for the Passover, forced to accompany Jesus along the way to the site of crucifixion, Golgotha, outside the city gates.

The soldiers offer wine mixed with myrrh. Was it an attempt to prolong Jesus' agony on the cross or mercy? Proverbs 31:6 says, "give beer to those who are perishing, wine to those who are in anguish, let them drink and forget their poverty and remember their misery no more." Jesus refuses, in keeping with his vow of abstinence at the Last Supper. The two men crucified with Jesus must have been rebels, like Barabbas: Rome did not crucify mere robbers. Myers writes that Mark, writing thirty-five to forty years after the crucifixion during the Jewish revolt against Rome, is "making a very important theological statement here." Mark has "dissociated Jesus from the means and ends of the rebel cause." Yet Jesus shares the rebel fate, "as common opponent" to Rome and the oppression of the people. Jesus has been traded for a murderer and will be crucified with two men of violence, who have the places of honor on Jesus' right and left sides, which the disciples fought for earlier.[5] They also taunt Jesus.

Mark's depiction of Jesus' solitary suffering has lived through the ages. As Tolbert notes,

> The period preceding his death when Jesus hangs on the cross is filled narratively, not by details of execution or physical pain, but by the taunting of an abusive, disdaining tide of humanity. It is Jesus' isolation and rejection that Mark emphasizes in the crucifixion. The fullness of suffering for the Gospel of Mark is the experience of being abandoned, left behind not only by all humanity but also by divinity. . . . For Mark, the most profound agony of the human spirit is not that engendered by the enmity of one's opponents but rather that caused by the betrayal and hatred of one's intimates. As Jesus declared early in his ministry, those who speak out for God are not despised *except* in their own homeland, among their own kin, and in their own houses. Moreover, the suffering brought about by separation, alienation, and isolation from family, homeland, and friends would strike a

familiar cord in the Greco-Roman world out of which the Gospel of Mark comes.... These cities, the breeding grounds for early Christianity ... offered their inhabitants no sense of community as citizens.[6]

Between the crucifixion and Mark's writing of the Gospel, there was periodic Roman persecution of Christians. During the reign of Caesar Nero, in Rome, Christians, torn apart by wild beasts, died in amphitheaters while the crowds cheered. Tacitus, the Roman historian, noted that derision accompanied their end. "Dressed in wild animals' skins, they were torn to pieces by dogs, or crucified or made into torches to be ignited after dark as substitutes for daylight."[7]

Suffering Christians over the centuries have identified with the agony of Jesus. The powerful African American spiritual "Were You There," which originated in the decades of American slavery, captures that identification for many of us.

> Were you there when they crucified my Lord?
> Were you there when they crucified my Lord?
> Oh! Sometimes it causes me to tremble, tremble, tremble.
> Were you there when they crucified my Lord?
>
> Were you there when they nailed him to the tree?
> Were you there when they nailed him to the tree?
> Oh! Sometimes it causes me to tremble, tremble, tremble.
> Were you there when they nailed him to the tree?
>
> Were you there when they pierced him in the side?
> Were you there when they pierced him in the side?
> Oh! Sometimes it causes me to tremble, tremble, tremble.
> Were you there when they pierced him in the side?
>
> Were you there when God raised him from the tomb?
> Were you there when God raised him from the tomb?
> Oh! Sometimes it causes me to tremble, tremble, tremble.
> Were you there when God raised him from the tomb?

Womanist theologian Raquel A. St. Clair writes that many black Americans, particularly black American women who have carried the triple burdens of classism, racism, and sexism, have seen Jesus as a "divine co-sufferer." Indeed, "during slavery, the suffering of Jesus on the cross was a mirror of the reality of their lives."[8] Suffering, shame, and surrogacy ("being forced or coerced to perform roles that normally belong to others"[9]) have been the legacy of the captive march onto the slave ships for the Middle Passage, slavery, reconstruction, and decades of discrimination, exploitation, and poverty. Scholars debate the number of Africans who died in the process of being made captive and in passage to the coast, in African confinement, in the Middle Passage from Africa to the Americas, and in the first few months in slavery in the Americas. Some place the figure as high as sixty million.

On a bluff overlooking the harbor of Morro da Cruz in Angola, from which millions of people were shipped as human cargo, stands a seventeenth-century church transformed into the National Slavery Museum. On one wall is a plaque in Portuguese with a reported 1967 quotation from Martin Luther King, Jr.: "we are descendents of slaves, we are offspring of men and women with dignity and honor." It is a haunting place with irons and implements of torture, old drawings and paintings of enslavement, carved wooden figures of children in chains, and carved wooden figures of women with babies and toddlers slung with fabric around their hips. The women's hands hold jute bundles and boxes upon their heads; chains around their necks connect one woman to the next. Enchained, forced to carry bundles for the slave-traders, and unable to reach to their children, the wooden suffering figures depict the triple burden with gut-wrenching force. They could not free themselves or their children.

The passers-by, chief priests, and scribes who mock Jesus on the cross, calling him to leave the cross and taunting him that he could save others but not himself, did not understand what it meant to be saved. To be saved is not to be safe; it is to be made whole, as the demoniac in the tombs, the hemorrhaging woman, and blind Bartimaeus were made whole. Belief in Jesus made broken, suffering people whole, as it did those Angolan Americans who sang, "Were you there when they crucified my Lord?" in the American South even as they plotted and worked for freedom from slavery. Belief in God, even though God seemed to have forsaken him, made Jesus whole, even as he hung broken on the cross.

Mark 15:33-39

[33]When it was noon, darkness came over the whole land until three in the afternoon. [34]At three o'clock Jesus cried out with a loud voice, "Eloi, Eloi, lema sabachthani?" which means, "My God, my God, why have you forsaken me?" [35]When some of the bystanders heard it, they said, "Listen, he is calling for Elijah." [36]And someone ran, filled a sponge with sour wine, put it on a stick, and gave it to him to drink, saying, "Wait, let us see whether Elijah will come to take him down." [37]Then Jesus gave a loud cry and breathed his last. [38]And the curtain of the temple was torn in two, from top to bottom. [39]Now when the centurion, who stood facing him, saw that in this way he breathed his last, he said, "Truly this man was God's Son!"

Jesus' cry echoes Psalm 22. Read the entire psalm aloud. The psalm begins in despair and ends in praise, triumph, and rejoicing! Was Jesus, in his final words, "My God, my God, why have you forsaken me?" trying to recite this psalm, which declares God's final victory?

This is the third apocalyptic scene in Mark.[10] The first was when the heavens were torn open and God's voice affirmed Jesus at his baptism. The second was on the mountain during the transformation when God's voice affirmed Jesus dressed in dazzling white, the clothing of a martyr. As Myers writes, this time God's "voice" is silent; however, there are two great symbols of God's judgment. The first is the sudden darkness over the land for three hours, similar to Exodus 10:22, "when Yahweh, in the war of myths with the pharaoh, blotted out the sun in Egypt for three days." The second is the tearing of the curtain of the temple, which Myers describes as "the apocalyptic unraveling of the whole cosmic order of domination, an unraveling promised by Jesus."[11] As Morna D. Hooker writes, Mark may have been thinking of the removal of a barrier between God and humanity, one that kept people from God's presence. "This is supported by the next verse where, astonishingly, the confession of faith is made by a gentile. If barriers are broken down, even gentiles can now enter."[12] It is a Roman soldier, indoctrinated that Caesar was the son of God, who proclaims that truly Jesus was the son of God.

Mark 15:40-47

⁴⁰There were also women looking on from a distance; among them were Mary Magdalene, and Mary the mother of James the younger and of Joses, and Salome. ⁴¹These used to follow him and provided for him when he was in Galilee; and there were many other women who had come up with him to Jerusalem. ⁴²When evening had come, and since it was the day of Preparation, that is, the day before the sabbath, ⁴³Joseph of Arimathea, a respected member of the council, who was also himself waiting expectantly for the kingdom of God, went boldly to Pilate and asked for the body of Jesus. ⁴⁴Then Pilate wondered if he were already dead; and summoning the centurion, he asked him whether he had been dead for some time. ⁴⁵When he learned from the centurion that he was dead, he granted the body to Joseph. ⁴⁶Then Joseph bought a linen cloth, and taking down the body, wrapped it in the linen cloth, and laid it in a tomb that had been hewn out of the rock. He then rolled a stone against the door of the tomb. ⁴⁷Mary Magdalene and Mary the mother of Joses saw where the body was laid.

The male disciples have fled; the women remain. Scholars have analyzed the Greek verbs to understand Mark's meaning of the women's activities.[13] As Japanese feminist Hisako Kinukawa writes, in the descriptions of "following," "provided for him,"[14] and "come up with him," Mark is presenting "key discipleship themes" and, indeed, is presenting the women as "model disciples."[15] They are "characterized as true disciples of Jesus who have left everything and have followed him on the way, even to its bitter end on the cross."[16] Was Jesus' mother among this group of named women or among the large group of unnamed women who Mark says followed him to Jerusalem and even to the cross? She could be the Mary identified as the mother of James and Joses, earlier named as brothers of Jesus.[17]

Why did Joseph of Arimathea intervene as he did? Myers sees him as acting as a member of the Sanhedrin, not out of compassion, but as one who did not want the corpse to profane the Sabbath.[18] Joseph gives Jesus' body a hasty burial, without the traditional rites and rituals of a Jewish burial. Others, however (and I am among them), understand Joseph to be acting out of respect and love, as quickly as he could before the Sabbath. Joseph was waiting for the kingdom. It took courage to go to Pilate; he went boldly and took the body down as an act of faith. It must have been a gruesome thing to remove a body from the cross: Joseph would have been covered with blood and wastes. It would have been a polluting act and certainly not the proper activity of a leading Jew. Is Mark's message that those who wait and work for the kingdom will pass through blood and pain? Again, the women are watching.

CHAPTER 19

MARK 16

Mark 16:1-8

¹When the sabbath was over, Mary Magdalene, and Mary the mother of James, and Salome bought spices, so that they might go and anoint him. ²And very early on the first day of the week, when the sun had risen, they went to the tomb. ³They had been saying to one another, "Who will roll away the stone for us from the entrance to the tomb?" ⁴When they looked up, they saw that the stone, which was very large, had already been rolled back. ⁵As they entered the tomb, they saw a young man, dressed in a white robe, sitting on the right side; and they were alarmed. ⁶But he said to them, "Do not be alarmed; you are looking for Jesus of Nazareth, who was crucified. He has been raised; he is not here. Look, there is the place they laid him. ⁷But go, tell his disciples and Peter that he is going ahead of you to Galilee; there you will see him, just as he told you." ⁸So they went out and fled from the tomb, for terror and amazement had seized them; and they said nothing to anyone, for they were afraid.

The women go as soon as they are able, when the Sabbath was over, for the mournful task of anointing for burial a corpse that would have already begun to decay and smell. Mark describes their world, however, as fresh and new: "very early on the first day of the week, when the sun had risen." Grieving, they do not have the eyes to see the ultimate reality and are not aware of the day's new life. First, they are anxious, worrying about the obstacle of the stone, and then seeing the young man, they are alarmed. The women see a "young man dressed in a white robe, sitting on the right side." The white robe is the symbol of martyrdom, and the right side is the place of true authority. Myers describes him as the "symbol of the transformation from betrayal (nakedness) to discipleship (white robe)," who issues the third call to discipleship.[1] The first call had been when Jesus said, "Come, follow me and I will make you fishers of men." The second was when he called to the crowd and his disciples and said, "If anyone would come after me, he must deny himself and take up his cross and follow me." Into the women's grief and the newness of early morning is the third call: "But go, tell his disciples and Peter, He is going ahead of you into Galilee. There you will see him, just as he told you." The women flee.

The ending to Mark's story can be puzzling. If the women said nothing to anyone, how do we know the story? Obviously they told the story! Schüssler Fiorenza, quoting D. Catchpole, interprets the women's flight as being flight from the tomb, but not flight from the young man's command "to tell his disciples and Peter." She writes,

> To be found at the tomb of someone executed was to risk being identified as his/her follower, and possibly even being arrested. The women's fear therefore was well founded. The statement that they kept silent because of this fear of being apprehended and executed like Jesus does not imply that they did not obey the command of the angel, however. "Generalized instruction to keep silence does not prevent disclosure to a specific individual (or group). It simply relates to the 'public at large.'" For instance in Mark 1:44 Jesus charges the healed leper: "See that you say nothing to anyone but go show yourself to the priest. . . ." The command to be silent does not exclude the information that must be given to the priest. Similarly, the silence of the women vis-à-vis the general public does not exclude fulfilling the command to "go and tell the disciples and Peter," and communicating the resurrected Lord's message of his going ahead to Galilee where they shall see him.[2]

Moreover, Mark's Gospel was written to be read or recited to Christian communities that knew the story of Jesus and the empty tomb. Mark's story is how to be a disciple in that context. To follow him as a disciple, having learned from his life and death, we must go to Galilee, the place of the margins, the outcast, and the rejected. Jerusalem, the "core" during Jesus' life, and the center of conflict in the Jewish rebellion when Mark was written, was not the place to encounter the Risen

Lord. We will see Jesus in Galilee where the story began. As Myers says, the narrative is circular. Back to Galilee—the hungry crowds, impoverished peasant villages, small family land holdings, broken day laborers, and estates of absentee landlords. Back to the conflict—the peasant 99 percent and the elite 1 percent. Back to the trauma, poverty, and oppression where Jesus healed, taught, and exorcised demons. Where the blind gained their sight and where the broken were made whole. Where the lame picked up their mats and walked. Where believers trusted enough to cut a hole in the roof of a house and lower a paralyzed man into Jesus' arms. Where a dead girl was given new life.

Mark's ending demands a response. Who will tell the good news? We now know the good news, as well as the women. What will we do? Myers writes, "Jesus is risen! But where has he gone? He is neither entombed (as the Romans think) nor enthroned (as the longer endings imagined). Mark refuses to show him to us. If we wish to see Jesus, we too must journey to Galilee. Jesus has gone ahead of the church. Only by responding to discipleship can we join him where he already is: on the way."[3]

In a village along the Nile River in Egypt, I met a woman who walked that road to Galilee. Sixteen hundred years ago, local Christians had sent missionaries to foreign lands, bishops to foundational Christian councils, and forged the monastic tradition that lives to this day throughout the world. Now, an impoverished area, it had the worst social welfare and health status in Egypt. Several miles down a dusty dirt road from the highway, the village sat among ancient irrigated fields, where farmers tilled crops as they did in Jesus' day. Above the doors of many of the poor, low, mud houses, a blue cross was painted, signifying that the family was Christian. I was there to evaluate the maternal health programs of the Coptic Orthodox Church, one clinic of which was several rooms attached to the village church.

The clinic was crowded with twenty-five women and children waiting for the doctor to arrive: Muslims in black burkas from head to toe, and Christians in bright clothes and scarves, with small blue crosses tattooed on their wrists since infancy (Illus. 19.1).

I waited with them in the 110-degree heat. The women reassured me, "Don't worry. She's late, but she'll come. She is faithful." Finally the doctor arrived—a fragile, sweaty, young woman in Western clothes

19.1 Egyptian women and children at a clinic

and high heels who had walked in from the highway. The village farmer who normally met her early in the morning for a ride behind him on his donkey had given up on her because her bus from the city was very late. Failing another alternative, in mid-morning as the temperature rose, she took off her high heels and walked to the clinic.

I asked her why she came all the way from the city to this little village. Female physicians were in great demand in this part of Egypt, and she could have had all the patients she wanted in the urban area from which she had come. She responded simply, "I am a Christian," held out her arm to show the blue wrist cross, and said, "These are my people." With a wave of her wrist encompassing the room, she said, "All of them, Christian and Muslim. Jesus is here among us. That's why I am here."

"CONFESSING CHRIST IN A WORLD OF VIOLENCE"*

In the October 2004 issue of *Sojourners*, Jim Wallis wrote of the dangers of American "righteous empire." Framed as a confession and signed by "more than 200 theologians and ethicists—many of them from theologically conservative seminaries and Christian colleges," it is a timeless witness to Jesus' teachings. In the introduction to the confession, Wallis wrote that he had joined with several other theologians and ethicists in writing "because of a deep and growing concern about an emerging 'theology of war' in the White House, the increasingly frequent language of 'righteous empire,' and official claims of 'divine appointment' for a nation and president in the 'war' on terrorism." He wrote, "A climate in which violence is too easily accepted, and the roles of God, church, and nation too easily confused calls for a new 'confession' of Christ." The following is that new confession.

> Our world is wracked with violence and war. But Jesus said: "Blessed are peacemakers, for they shall be called the children of God" (Matt. 5:9). Innocent people, at home and abroad, are increasingly threatened by terrorist attacks. But Jesus said: "Love your enemies, pray for those who persecute you" (Matt. 5:44). These words, which have never been easy, seem all the more difficult today. Nevertheless, a time comes when silence is betrayal. How many churches have heard sermons on these texts since the terrorist atrocities of September 11? Where is the serious debate about what it means to confess Christ in a world of violence?

---

*Jim Wallis, "A New Confession of Christ," *Sojourners* (October 2004): http://www.sojourners.com/sojomail/2004/10/20. This is an abridged version of the original article, reprinted with permission from Sojourners (800-714-7474). For the full version of this article, please visit www.sojo.net.

Does Christian "realism" mean resigning ourselves to an endless future of "pre-emptive wars"? Does it mean turning a blind eye to torture and massive civilian casualties? Does it mean acting out of fear and resentment rather than intelligence and restraint?

Faithfully confessing Christ is the church's task, and never more so than when its confession is co-opted by militarism and nationalism. . . . The security issues before our nation allow no easy solutions. No one has a monopoly on the truth. But a policy that rejects the wisdom of international consultation should not be baptized by religiosity. The danger today is political idolatry exacerbated by the politics of fear. In this time of crisis, we need a new confession of Christ.

1. Jesus Christ, as attested in Holy Scripture, knows no national boundaries. Those who confess his name are found throughout the earth. Our allegiance to Christ takes priority over national identity. Whenever Christianity compromises with empire, the gospel of Christ is discredited. We reject the false teaching that any nation-state can ever be described with the words, "the light shines in the darkness and the darkness has not overcome it." These words, used in scripture, apply only to Christ. No political or religious leader has the right to twist them in the service of war.

2. Christ commits Christians to a strong presumption against war. The wanton destructiveness of modern warfare strengthens this obligation. Standing in the shadow of the Cross, Christians have a responsibility to count the cost, speak out for the victims, and explore every alternative before a nation goes to war. We are committed to international cooperation rather than unilateral policies. We reject the false teaching that a war on terrorism takes precedence over ethical and legal norms. Some things ought never be done—torture, the deliberate bombing of civilians, the use of indiscriminate weapons of mass destruction—regardless of the consequences.

3. Christ commands us to see not only the splinter in our adversary's eye, but also the beam in our own. The distinction between

good and evil does not run between one nation and another, or one group and another. It runs straight through every human heart. We reject the false teaching that America is a "Christian nation," representing only virtue, while its adversaries are nothing but vicious. We reject the belief that America has nothing to repent of, even as we reject that it represents most of the world's evil. All have sinned and fallen short of the glory of God (Rom. 3:23).

4. Christ shows us that enemy-love is the heart of the gospel. While we were yet enemies, Christ died for us (Rom. 5:8, 10). We are to show love to our enemies even as we believe God in Christ has shown love to us and the whole world. Enemy-love does not mean capitulating to hostile agendas or domination. It does mean refusing to demonize any human being created in God's image. We reject the false teaching that any human being can be defined as outside the law's protection. We reject the demonization of perceived enemies, which only paves the way to abuse; and we reject the mistreatment of prisoners, regardless of supposed benefits to their captors.

5. Christ teaches us that humility is the virtue befitting forgiven sinners. It tempers all political disagreements, and it allows that our own political perceptions, in a complex world, may be wrong. We reject the false teaching that those who are not for the USA politically are against it or that those who fundamentally question American policies must be with the "evil-doers." Such crude distinctions, especially when used by Christians, are expressions of the Manichaean heresy, in which the world is divided into forces of absolute good and absolute evil.

The Lord Jesus Christ is either authoritative for Christians, or he is not. His Lordship cannot be set aside by any earthly power. His words may not be distorted for propagandistic purposes. No nation-state may usurp the place of God. We believe that acknowledging these truths is indispensable for followers of Christ. We urge them to remember these principles in making their decisions as citizens. Peacemaking is central to our vocation in a troubled world where Christ is Lord.

ENDNOTES

Introduction

1. Ched Myers, *Binding the Strong Man: A Political Reading of Mark's Story of Jesus* (Maryknoll, NY: Orbis Books, 2002).

2. William Herzog II, *Parables as Subversive Speech: Jesus as Pedagogue of the Oppressed* (Louisville: Westminster John Knox, 1994).

3. Elisabeth Schüssler Fiorenza, *In Memory of Her: A Feminist Theological Reconstruction of Christian Origins* (New York: Crossroad, 2002), 102.

4. Barry R. Posen, "Command of the Commons, The Military Foundation of U.S. Hegemony," *International Security* 28, no. 1 (Summer 2003), 10.

5. Otto Maduro, "Once Again Liberating Theology: Towards a Latin American Liberation Theological Self-Criticism," in *Liberation Theology and Sexuality,* ed. Marcella Althaus-Reid (London: SCM Press, 2009), 25.

6. Schüssler Fiorenza, *In Memory of Her,* 107.

Chapter 1 • Empire in First-Century Palestine

1. Charles S. Maier, *Among Empires* (Cambridge, MA: Harvard University Press, 2006), 7.

2. John Dominic Crossan, quoting Mann in "Roman Imperial Theology," in *In the Shadow of Empire,* ed. Richard Horsley (Louisville: Westminster John Knox, 2008), 60.

3. Speech ascribed to the British rebel general Calgacus by Roman historian Tacitus in his *Agricola* 30, quoted in John Dominic Crossan, *Jesus: A Revolutionary Biography* (San Francisco: HarperSanFrancisco, 1989), 39.

4. Gerhard Lenski, *Power and Privilege: A Theory of Social Stratification* (New York: McGraw Hill, 1966), 52.

5. John Dominic Crossan, "Roman Imperial Theology," 60.

6. *Res Gestae divi Augusti, The Achievements of the Divine Augustus,* ed. P. A. Brunt and J. M. Moore (New York: Oxford University Press, 1967), 19-37.

Chapter 2 • Palestine in the First Century

1. Sean Freyne, *Jesus, A Jewish Galilean: A New Reading of the Jesus Story* (London: T&T Clark International, 2004), 52.

2. Ibid., 134.

3. Gerd Theissen, *The Gospels in Context: Social and Political History in the Synoptic Tradition* (Edinburgh: T&T Clark, 1992), 68-75.

4. Ibid., 75.

5. In the andocentric literature of the time, there is no documentation on maternal mortality; however, basic female anatomy and physiology have not changed in the last two thousand years, and early and frequent childbirth is directly correlated with maternal and infant mortality. Malnutrition and heavy labor would have exacerbated the problem, leading to premature births, low birth weights, and infant and maternal illness and death.

6. Israel Finkelstein and Neil Asher Silberman, *The Bible Unearthed* (New York: Free Press, 2001), 247.

7. Walter Brueggemann, *Journey to the Common Good* (Louisville: Westminster John Knox, 2010), 38.

8. Shaye J. D. Cohen, *From the Maccabees to the Mishnah* (Louisville: Westminster John Knox, 2006), 192.

9. Wes Howard-Brook, *"Come Out, My People": God's Call out of Empire in the Bible and Beyond* (Maryknoll, NY: Orbis Books, 2010), 372.

10. Richard A. Horsley, "Jesus and Empire," in *In the Shadow of Empire,* ed. Richard Horsley (Louisville: Westminster John Knox, 2008), 80.

11. William R. Herzog II, *Jesus, Justice and the Reign of God* (Louisville: Westminster John Knox, 2000), 149.

12. Horsley, "Jesus and Empire," 80.

13. Herzog, *Jesus, Justice and the Reign of God,* 137.

14. Richard A. Horsley, *Bandits, Prophets and Messiahs* (Harrisburg, PA: Trinity Press International, 1985), 54-55.

15. Herzog, *Jesus, Justice and the Reign of God,* 137.

16. Ched Myers, *Binding the Strong Man: A Political Reading of Mark's Story of Jesus* (Maryknoll, NY: Orbis Books), 73-75.

17. Herzog, *Jesus, Justice and the Reign of God,* 150.

18. Brueggemann, *Journey to the Common Good,* 38-39.

19. Howard-Brook, *"Come Out, My People,"* 170.

20. Ibid., 162.

21. There may have been three authors of the book we call Isaiah, writing at the three critical times in the book: before, during, and after the Babylonian Exile. Likewise, scholars detect multiple authorial voices and time periods in the book of Micah. However, the emphasis on justice and righteousness is constant.

22. William R. Herzog II, *Prophet and Teacher: An Introduction to the Historical Jesus* (Louisville: Westminster John Knox, 2005), 51-53.

23. Richard A. Horsley, *Jesus and Empire* (Minneapolis: Fortress Press, 2003), 53.

24. Other resistance texts were Daniel and the Psalms of Solomon.

25. Howard-Brook, *"Come Out, My People,"* 374-76.

26. Horsley, *Jesus and Empire,* 49-54.

27. Herzog, *Prophet and Teacher,* 193.

28. Horsley, *Jesus and Empire,* 29.

29. Robert J. Miller, *The Complete Gospels* (Santa Rosa, CA: Polebridge Press, 1994), 10.

Chapter 3 • Empire Today

1. Diane Brady and Christopher Palmeri, "The Pet Economy," *Businessweek* (August 6, 2007): www.businessweek.com/magazine/content/07_32/b4045001. htm.

2. *Consumer Reports,* "Holiday Spending 2010" (November 4, 2010): http: // onlocation.consumerreports.org/tv/index.cfm?storydate=2010-12&storynumber= 14&station=w123.

3. National Mail Order Association, "Final Pre-Christmas Push Propels U.S. Online Holiday Season Spending through December 26 to Record $30.8 Billion" (December 29, 2010): www.comscore.com/por/layout/set/popup/Press_Events/ Press_Releases/2010/12/Final_Pre_Christmas_Push_Propels_U.S._Online_ Holiday_Season_Spending.

4. James B. Davies, Susanna Sandstrom, Anthony Schorrocks, and Edward N. Wolff, "The World Distribution of Household Wealth," in *Personal Wealth from a Global Perspective,* ed. James B. Davies (Oxford: Oxford University Press, 2008), 405.

5. Carmen DeNavas-Walt, Bernadette D. Proctor, and Jessica C. Smith, *Income, Poverty, and Health Insurance Coverage in the USA: 2010* (U.S. Census Bureau, Current Population Reports: Washington, DC: U.S. Government Printing Office, 2011), 14. These figures do not include the value of subsidized housing, food stamps, and other forms of national and state assistance to the poor. From 1959 to 2010 the U.S. population increased by 74 percent. There has been a decrease in the percentage of those in poverty and an increase in the absolute numbers of those in poverty, due in part, undoubtedly to the population increase.

6. Albert Crenshaw, "Gap between Rich and Poor Grows," *Washington Post,* January 22, 2003.

7. James B. Davies, Susanna Sandstrom, Anthony Schorrocks, and Edward N. Wolff, "The Level and Distribution of Global Household Wealth," *Economic Journal* 121 (March 2011), 223-54.

8. Rakesh Kochhar, Richard Fry, and Paul Taylor, "Wealth Gaps Rise to Record Highs between Whites, Blacks and Hispanics," Pew Social and Demographic Trends, Pew Research Center (July 26, 2011): www.pewsocialtrends.org/2011/07/26/wealth-gaps-rise-to-record-highs-between-whites-blacks-hispanics, 1.

9. Ibid.

10. Ronald Sider, *Just Generosity: A New Vision for Overcoming Poverty in America* (Grand Rapids, MI: Baker Books, 2007), 54.

11. Rhode Island Community Food Bank, Statistics (August 30, 2011): www. rifoodbank.org/matriarch/MultiPiecePage.asp_Q_PageID_E_31_A_PageName_E_ StatsThermometerGraphic.

12. Susan B. Epstein and Matthew C. Weed, *Foreign Aid Reform: Studies and Recommendations* (Washington, DC: Congressional Research Service, September 28, 2009): www.fas.org/sgp/crs/row/R40102.pdf.

13. Shirl Arthur, "A Conservative Estimate of Total Direct U.S. Aid to Israel: Almost $114 Billion," *Washington Report on Middle Eastern Affairs,* November 2008.

14. Andrew J. Shapiro, "The Obama Administration's Approach to U.S. Security Cooperation: Preserving Israel's Qualitative Military Edge" (July 26, 2010): www.state.gov/t/pm/rls/rm/144753.htm.

15. Epstein and Weed, *Foreign Aid Reform.*

16. "U.S. Government Foreign Grants and Credits by Country: 2000 to 2008": www.census.gov/compendia/statab/2010/tables/10s1261.pdf.

17. National Research Council and Institute of Medicine, *U.S. Health in International Perspective: Shorter Lives, Poorer Health*, Panel on Understanding Cross-National Health Differences among High-Income Countries, ed. Steven H. Woolf and Laudan Aron, Committee on Population, Division of Behavioral and Social Sciences and Education, and Board on Population Health and Public Health Practice, Institute of Medicine (Washington, DC: National Academies Press, 2013).

18. Ibid., 40.

19. Ibid., 89.

20. Ibid., 185.

21. "Women in the lowest income category experience more than six times the rate of nonfatal intimate partner violence as compared to women in the highest income category. See National Organization for Women, "Violence against Women in the United States: Statistics" (December 2011): www.now.org/issues/violence/stats.html.

22. Personal interview with United Methodist Rev. Santos Escobar of Providence, RI, 2007.

23. United Nations Human Development Report, 2009, *Overcoming Barriers: Human Mobility and Development* (New York: HRD, 2009), http://hdr.undp.org, front piece.

24. The EB-5 programs grant green cards to foreign investors and their families with at least a $500,000 investment in the United States that generates ten jobs. Other First World governments also strictly control immigration.

25. Chalmers Johnson, *Dismantling the Empire: America's Last Best Hope* (New York: Metropolitan Books, Henry Holt, 2010), 12-13.

26. Ibid.

27. Barry R. Posen, "Command of the Commons, The Military Foundation of U.S. Hegemony," *International Security* 28, no. 1 (Summer 2003), 5-46.

28. Ibid., 10.

29. Ibid., 9.

30. Department of Defense, "Base Structure Report, FY 2009 Baseline" (December 2011): www.acq.osd.mil/ie/download/bsr/BSR2009Baseline.pdf.

31. Johnson, *Dismantling the Empire*, 121.

32. The Stockholm International Peace Research Institute (SIPRI) (April 2011),

"Background Paper on SIPRI Military Expenditure Data, 2010": www.sipri.org/research/armaments/milex/factsheet2010.

33. Elisabeth Bumiller, "The War: A Trillion Can Be Cheap," *New York Times*, July 24, 2010.

34. Ibid.

35. Posen, "Command of the Commons," 7.

36. In Kenya as a whole, the AIDS prevalence was 13.5 percent.

37. Nermeen Al-Mufti, "In the Rubble of Falluja," *Al-Ahram Weekly*, December 3, 2004. I was in Egypt at the time.

38. UNHCR Fact Sheet (August 2010): www.iauiraq.org/documents/1073/1_Fact%20sheet%20August%202010E.pdf.

39. Joseph E. Stiglitz and Linda J. Bilmes, *The Three Trillion Dollar War* (New York: W. W. Norton, 2008), 10-11.

40. Jim Wallis, *God's Politics: Why the Right Gets It Wrong and the Left Doesn't Get It* (New York: Harper Collins, 2005), 147.

Chapter 4 • Mark 1

1. Although Mark says he quotes Isaiah, in fact the quotation is a combination of Malachi 3:1 and Isaiah 40:3-5, both excerpts from larger Hebrew scriptures proclaiming God's righteousness and faithfulness.

2. Walter Brueggemann, *Journey to the Common Good* (Louisville: Westminster John Knox, 2010), 89.

3. Ched Myers, *Binding the Strong Man: A Political Reading of Mark's Story of Jesus* (Maryknoll, NY: Orbis Books, 2002), 124.

4. Brueggemann, *Journey to the Common Good,* 15.

5. Paul R. McReynolds, *Word Study Greek-English New Testament* (Wheaton, IL: Tyndale, 1990), 122.

6. Scholars believe that behind today's languages of peoples from Europe to India lies a common ancestral language (Indo-European) that was spoken in Europe and Asia six thousand years ago. This ancestral language is the root for the Latin, Greek, and Aramaic of two thousand years ago as well as for the English, French, and Spanish of today. One can search many modern words back to their early roots to understand their meaning in Palestine in the first century. To find the Indo-European root of a word, look the word up in a comprehensive dictionary with Indo-European roots in the appendix.

7. Walter Wink, *Unmasking the Powers: The Invisible Forces That Determine Human Existence* (Philadelphia: Fortress Press, 1986), 14.

8. Wink, *Unmasking the Powers,* 14.

9. Ibid., 10.

10. Ibid., 104.

11. Ibid.

12. Dr. Martin Luther King, "Where Do We Go from Here?," Address to the Southern Christian Leadership Conference (August 16, 1967).

13. Sean Freyne, *Jesus, A Jewish Galilean: A New Reading of the Jesus Story* (London: T&T Clark International, 2004), 52

14. Elisabeth Schüssler Fiorenza, *In Memory of Her* (New York: Crossroad, 2002), 102.

15. Ben Witherington, *Gospel of Mark: A Socio-Rhetorical Commentary* (Grand Rapids, MI: William B. Eerdmans, 2001), 88.

16. David Rhodes, *Reading Mark, Engaging the Gospel* (Minneapolis: Fortress Press, 2004), 154-55.

17. Sharon G. Thornton, *Broken yet Beloved: A Pastoral Theology of the Cross* (St. Louis: Chalice Press, 2002), 195.

18. William R. Herzog II, *Parables as Subversive Speech: Jesus as Pedagogue of the Oppressed* (Louisville: Westminster John Knox, 1994).

19. Ched Myers, *Say to This Mountain* (Maryknoll, NY: Orbis Books, 2003), 14.

20. Ibid., 15.

21. Robert J. Miller, *Complete Gospels* (Santa Rosa, CA: Polebridge Press, 1994), 456.

22. Myers, *Binding the Strong Man*, 37.

23. Thornton, *Broken yet Beloved*, 73.

24. Walter Brueggemann, *Praying the Psalms* (Eugene, OR: Cascade Books, 2007), 8.

25. Ibid., 16.

26. William R. Herzog II, *Prophet and Teacher: An Introduction to the Historical Jesus* (Louisville: Westminster John Knox, 2005), 21.

27. William Barclay, *The Gospel of Mark* (Louisville: Westminster John Knox, 2001), 50.

28. Schüssler Fiorenza, *In Memory of Her*, 131.

29. Myers, *Binding the Strong Man*, 153.

Chapter 5 • Mark 2

1. World Health Organization, "Children: Reducing Mortality," Fact Sheet no. 178 (October 2011): www.who.int/mediacentre/factsheets/fs178/en/index.html.

2. N. T. Wright, *Jesus and the Victory of God* (Minneapolis: Fortress Press 1996), 276.

3. Wright, *Jesus and the Victory of God*, 110.

4. William R. Herzog II, *Prophet and Teacher: An Introduction to the Historical Jesus* (Louisville: Westminster John Knox, 2005), 80-81.

5. Ched Myers, *Binding the Strong Man: A Political Reading of Mark's Story of Jesus* (Maryknoll, NY: Orbis Books, 2002), 156.

6. Rakesh Kochhar, Richard Fry, and Paul Taylor, "Wealth Gaps Rise to Record

Highs between Whites, Blacks and Hispanics" (Pew Social and Demographic Trends, Pew Research Center, July 26, 2011): www.pewsocialtrends.org/2011/07/26/wealth-gaps-rise-to-record-highs-between-whites-blacks-hispanics, 1.

Chapter 6 • Mark 3

1. Ched Myers, *Say to This Mountain* (Maryknoll, NY: Orbis Books, 2003), 26.
2. Ibid., 32.
3. Rollo May, *Love and Will* (New York: W.W. Norton, 1969), 168.
4. Myers, *Say to This Mountain*, 32.
5. Elisabeth Schüssler Fiorenza, *In Memory of Her* (New York: Crossroad, 2002), 30.
6. Walter Wink, *Unmasking the Powers: The Invisible Forces That Determine Human Existence* (Philadelphia: Fortress Press, 1986), 105.
7. Quoted in Ched Myers, *Binding the Strong Man: A Political Reading of Mark's Story of Jesus* (Maryknoll, NY: Orbis Books, 2002), 167.
8. Schüssler Fiorenza, *In Memory of Her*, 147.

Chapter 7 • Mark 4

1. Walter Brueggemann, *Theology of the Old Testament* (Minneapolis: Fortress Press 1997), 153.
2. William R. Herzog II, *Parables as Subversive Speech: Jesus as Pedagogue of the Oppressed* (Louisville: Westminster John Knox, 1994), 27.
3. William R. Herzog II, "The Sower," personal communication, 2010.
4. Go to their website and see the remarkable videos of wholeness and new life at http://ginghamsburg.org/sudan/.
5. Ched Myers, *Say to This Mountain* (Maryknoll, NY: Orbis Books, 2003), 42.
6. Ibid., 43-44.
7. http://www.jamkhed.org.
8. Myers, *Say to This Mountain*, 57.

Chapter 8 • Mark 5

1. Gerd Theissen, The *Gospels in Context: Social and Political History in the Synoptic Tradition* (Edinburgh: T&T Clark, 1992), 110.
2. Ched Myers, *Say to This Mountain* (Maryknoll, NY: Orbis Books, 2003), 58-59.
3. Ibid., 59.
4. Franz Fanon, *Wretched of the Earth* (New York: Grove Press, 1963).
5. Based on conversations I had with a number of people in El Salvador in 2002.
6. Myers, *Say to This Mountain*, 63.
7. Ibid.
8. Karen Jo Torjesen, "Reconstruction of Women's Early Christian History," in *Searching the Scriptures*, vol. 1, ed. Elisabeth Schüssler Fiorenza (New York: Crossroad, 1993), 291.

9. Mary Ann Tolbert, "Mark," in *Women's Bible Commentary,* ed. Carol A. Newsom and Sharon H. Ringe (Louisville: Westminster John Knox, 1998), 352.

10. John R. Donahue and Daniel J. Harrington, *The Gospel of Mark* (Collegeville, MN: Liturgical Press, 2002), 177.

Chapter 9 • Mark 6

1. Halvor Moxnes, *Putting Jesus in His Place* (Louisville: Westminster John Knox, 2003), 2.

2. Ibid., 53.

3. Ched Myers, *Binding the Strong Man: A Political Reading of Mark's Story of Jesus* (Maryknoll, NY: Orbis Books, 2002), 213.

4. Mary Ann Tolbert, *Sowing the Gospel: Mark's World in Literary-Historical Perspective* (Minneapolis: Fortress Press, 1996), 197-98.

5. Myers, *Binding the Strong Man,* 215-16.

6. Rhode Island Coalition for the Homeless, Press Release (December 19, 2012), www.rihomeless.org/Portals/0/Uploads/Documents/Winter%20shelter%20release 12.pdf.

7. John R. Donahue and Daniel J. Harrington, *The Gospel of Mark* (Collegeville, MN: Liturgical Press, 2002), 213.

8. Harm de Blij, *The Power of Place: Geography, Destiny, and Globalization's Rough Landscape* (New York: Oxford University Press, 2009), 14-15.

9. Divestment Task Force, "Company Summaries" (New England Conference United Methodist Church, May 2010): www.neumc.org/pages/detail/375.

10. For further information on the New England United Methodist Task Force and a list of twenty-nine multinational companies that profit from the occupation either by "Providing support for the occupation's infrastructure (settlements, roads, checkpoints, or portions of the separation wall built on occupied land); having a physical presence such as a factory or store on occupied land, or providing the Israeli military with offensive weapons or items used to enforce the occupation of Palestinian land." See: www.neumc.org/console/files/oFiles_Library_XZXLCZ/Companies_ Recommended_for_Divestment_HJKKVNTP.pdf.

Chapter 10 • Mark 7

1. Jodi Magness, *Stone and Dung, Oil and Spit, Jewish Daily Life in the Time of Jesus* (Grand Rapids, MI: William B. Eerdmans, 2011), 18.

2. David Rhoades, *Reading Mark, Engaging the Gospel* (Minneapolis: Fortress Press, 2004), 83-85.

3. Elisabeth Schüssler Fiorenza, *But She Said: Feminist Practices of Biblical Interpretation* (Boston: Beacon Press, 1992), 160-63.

4. Ibid.,163.

5. Ibid., 97.

6. Ibid., 162.

7. Rhodes, *Reading Mark,* 231.
8. Ibid., 84.

Chapter 11 • Mark 8

1. For more information on Fair Trade coffee, tea, and chocolate, see http://fairtrade.net/.
2. John R. Donahue and Daniel J. Harrington, *The Gospel of Mark* (Collegeville, MN: Liturgical Press, 2002), 248.
3. Donahue and Harrington, *The Gospel of Mark,* 252.
4. Jeffrey Gettleman, "Leaked Fuel Lures Needy Kenyans, Then Ignites," *New York Times,* September 12, 2011.
5. Sean Freyne, *Jesus, A Jewish Galilean: A New Reading of the Jesus Story* (London: T&T Clark International, 2004), 134.
6. Qumran was the site of another first-century Jewish renewal movement; the Romans destroyed the movement and site during the Roman-Jewish war of 66–73 C.E. Scrolls were found in a cave 1,900 years later. The *Psalms of Solomon* were among the Dead Sea Scrolls, also found in the last century. The *Parables of Enoch,* a first-century B.C.E. writing, are in the Ethiopian text of *1 Enoch,* a Jewish pseudepigraphal writing.
7. Bruce J. Malina, *The New Testament World: Insights from Cultural Anthropology* (Louisville: Westminster John Knox, 2001), 30.
8. Ibid., 49
9. Ched Myers, *Say to This Mountain* (Maryknoll, NY: Orbis Books, 2003), 103.
10. Eunice K. Y. Or, "Thousands Mourn American Nun Murdered in Amazon for Advocacy Work," *Christianity Today* (February 16, 2005).

Chapter 12 • Mark 9

1. John R. Donahue and Daniel J. Harrington, *The Gospel of Mark* (Collegeville, MN: Liturgical Press, 2002), 270-71.
2. Ched Myers, *Say to This Mountain* (Maryknoll, NY: Orbis Books, 2003), 112.
3. Donahue and Harrington, *The Gospel of Mark,* 288-89.

Chapter 13 • Mark 10

1. Elisabeth Schüssler Fiorenza, *In Memory of Her: A Feminist Theological Reconstruction of Christian Origins* (New York: Crossroad, 2002), 143.
2. Ibid., 143.
3. Ched Myers, *Binding the Strong Man: A Political Reading of Mark's Story of Jesus* (Maryknoll, NY: Orbis Books, 2002), 266.
4. Paul R. McReynolds, *Word Study Greek-English New Testament* (Wheaton, IL: Tyndale, 1990), 165.
5. Lamar Williamson, Jr., *Mark* (Louisville: John Knox, 1983), 183.
6. James B. Davies, Susanna Sandstrom, Anthony Schorrocks, and Edward N. Wolff, "The Level and Distribution of Global Household Wealth," *Economic Journal* 121 (March 2011), 223-54.

7. Dr. Martin Luther King, Jr., Letter from a Birmingham Jail, April 16, 1963.

8. Mary Potter Engel, "Evil, Sin and the Violation of the Vulnerable," in *Constructing Christian Theologies from the Underside,* ed. Susan Brooks Thistlethwaite and Mary Potter Engel (San Francisco: HarperSanFrancisco, 1990), 160.

9. Richard Horsley, *Jesus and the Spiral of Violence* (Minneapolis: Fortress Press, 1993), 244-45.

10. Kenneth E. Bailey, *Jesus through Middle Eastern Eyes* (Downers Grove, IL: IVP Academic, 2008), 170-74.

11. Williamson, *Mark*, 197-98.

Chapter 14 • Mark 11

1. Lamar Williamson, Jr., *Mark* (Louisville: John Knox, 1983), 203.

2. Marcus Borg, *The Gospel of Mark: Conversations with Scripture* (Harrisburg, PA: Morehouse Publishing, 2009), 91.

3. Williamson, *Mark*, 203.

4. John R. Donahue and Daniel J. Harrington, *The Gospel of Mark* (Collegeville, MN: Liturgical Press, 2002), 325.

5. Ched Myers, *Binding the Strong Man: A Political Reading of Mark's Story of Jesus* (Maryknoll, NY: Orbis Books, 2002), 298-99.

6. Donahue and Harrington, *The Gospel of Mark*, 327.

7. William R. Herzog II, *Jesus, Justice and the Reign of God* (Louisville: Westminster John Knox, 2000), 137.

8. Ibid., 141.

9. Myers, *Binding the Strong Man*, 305.

10. Ibid., 306-7.

11. David Rhodes, *Reading Mark, Engaging the Gospel* (Minneapolis: Fortress Press, 2004), 86.

Chapter 15 • Mark 12

1. William R. Herzog II, *Parables as Subversive Speech: Jesus as Pedagogue of the Oppressed* (Louisville: Westminster John Knox, 1994), 3.

2. Ibid., 27-28.

3. Ibid., 102.

4. Ibid., 109-10.

5. Ibid., 84.

6. Ched Myers, *Binding the Strong Man: A Political Reading of Mark's Story of Jesus* (Maryknoll, NY: Orbis Books, 2002), 315.

7. Elisabeth Schüssler Fiorenza, *In Memory of Her: A Feminist Theological Reconstruction of Christian Origins* (New York: Crossroad, 2002), 144.

8. Myers, *Binding the Strong Man*, 318.

9. Ibid., 319.

10. Ibid., 320.

11. Linda Bloom, "Bolivian Methodists Join Push for Justice" (UMC News Archives, June 2005): http://archives.umc.org/interior.asp?ptid=1&mid=9193.

Chapter 16 • Mark 13

1. Ched Myers, *Say to This Mountain* (Maryknoll, NY: Orbis Books, 2003), 174.
2. To differentiate it from John's Revelation, which is the major first-century Christian apocalyptic text.
3. Myers, *Say to This Mountain*, 170-71.
4. Mary Ann Tolbert, "When Resistance Becomes Repression," in *Reading from this Place*, vol. 2, ed. Fernando F. Segovia and Mary Ann Tolbert (Minneapolis: Fortress Press, 1995), 336.
5. Quoted in Ched Myers, *Binding the Strong Man: A Political Reading of Mark's Story of Jesus* (Maryknoll, NY: Orbis Books, 2002), 322.
6. William R. Herzog II, *Jesus, Justice and the Reign of God* (Louisville: Westminster John Knox, 2000), 143.
7. Paul L. Maier, *Josephus: The Essential Works* (Grand Rapids, MI: Kregel Publications, 1998), 376.

Chapter 17 • Mark 14

1. Elisabeth Schüssler Fiorenza, *In Memory of Her: A Feminist Theological Reconstruction of Christian Origins* (New York: Crossroad, 2002), 153.
2. Ibid. She dates that loss of solidarity to the time of the Gospel of Luke, about 95 C.E.
3. In a murderous civil war that pitted the legitimate demands of the poor for economic justice against the few wealthy families who owned the country, the government supported the status quo and targeted the Roman Catholic Church for its consciousness raising with the peasants.
4. John R. Donahue and Daniel J. Harrington, *The Gospel of Mark* (Collegeville, MN: Liturgical Press, 2002), 412
5. Raymond E. Brown, *The Death of the Messiah*, vol. 1 (New Haven: Yale University Press, 1994), 266-67.
6. Brown, *The Death of the Messiah*, 298.
7. Gerd Theissen, *The Gospels in Context: Social and Political History in the Synoptic Tradition* (Edinburgh: T&T Clark, 1992), 186-87.
8. Congressional Research Service, quoted in the *New York Times*, September 11, 2011.
9. Margaret Griffis, "Causalities in Iraq" (antiwar.com, December 2011): http://antiwar.com/casualties.
10. Dale Keiger, "The Number," *Johns Hopkins Magazine* (February 2007): 30-37.
11. Sharon G. Thornton, *Broken yet Beloved: A Pastoral Theology of the Cross* (St. Louis: Chalice Press, 2002), 76.
12. William R. Herzog II, *Jesus, Justice and the Reign of God* (Louisville: Westminster John Knox, 2000), 218.
13. Brown, *The Death of the Messiah*, 497.

Chapter 18 • Mark 15

1. Ched Myers, *Say to This Mountain* (Maryknoll, NY: Orbis Books, 2003), 194.

2. Other Gospels give an even more lenient picture of the man, contrary to the historical record.

3. Ched Myers, *Binding the Strong Man: A Political Reading of Mark's Story of Jesus* (Maryknoll, NY: Orbis Books, 2002), 374.

4. Barabbas may have been a member of the Zealots, a Jewish revolutionary group, which began about 3 c.e., fought the Romans in the civil war of 66–70, and then as part of a remnant of about one thousand men, women, and children retreated to the mountain fortress of Masada. After holding out against the Romans, the majority committed mass suicide in 73 c.e. rather than surrender to the Romans.

5. Myers, *Binding the Strong Man*, 387.

6. Mary Ann Tolbert, "Mark," in *Women's Bible Commentary,* ed. Carol A. Newsom and Sharon H. Ringe (Louisville: Westminster John Knox, 1998), 286-87.

7. Cornelius Tacitus, *The Annals of Imperial Rome* (London: Penguin Books, 1956), 365.

8. Raquel A. St. Clair, *Call and Consequences* (Minneapolis: Fortress Press, 2008), 4-5.

9. Ibid., 25.

10. Myers, *Say to This Mountain*, 200.

11. Ibid., 389-90.

12. Morna D. Hooker, *The Gospel According to Saint Mark* (Peabody, MA: Hendrickson Publishers, 2009), 378.

13. See Elisabeth Schüssler Fiorenza, *In Memory of Her: A Feminist Theological Reconstruction of Christian Origins* (New York: Crossroad, 2002), 320-22; and Hisako Kinukawa, "Women Disciples of Jesus (15.40-41; 15.47; 16.1)," in *A Feminist Companion of Mark*, ed. Amy-Jill Levine (Cleveland: Pilgrim Press, 2001), 177-78.

14. Translated as "served" in many Bible translations.

15. Hisako Kinukawa, "Women Disciples of Jesus," 178.

16. Schüssler Fiorenza, *In Memory of Her*, 320.

17. Hisako Kinukawa, "Women Disciples of Jesus," 173. Other Gospels identify Mary by name as being among the group.

18. Myers, *Binding the Strong Man*, 394-96.

Chapter 19 • Mark 16

1. Ched Myers, *Say to This Mountain* (Maryknoll, NY: Orbis Books, 2003), 207.

2. Elisabeth Schüssler Fiorenza, *In Memory of Her: A Feminist Theological Reconstruction of Christian Origins* (New York: Crossroad, 2002), 322.

3. Myers, *Say to This Mountain*, 209.

Index